HOW TO MAKE $100,000 A YEAR AS A PRIVATE INVESTIGATOR

EDMUND J. PANKAU
CLI, CPP, CFE

PALADIN PRESS
BOULDER, COLORADO

How to Make $100,000 a Year as a Private Investigator
by Edmund J. Pankau

Copyright © 1993 by Edmund J. Pankau

ISBN 10: 0-87364-720-3
ISBN 13: 978-0-87364-720-5

Printed in the United States of America

Published by Paladin Press, a division of
Paladin Enterprises, Inc.
Gunbarrel Tech Center
7077 Winchester Circle
Boulder, Colorado 80301 USA
+1.303.443.7250

Direct inquiries and/or orders to the above address.

Visit our Web site at www.paladin-press.com

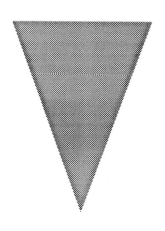

Contents

Foreword		vii
Introduction		1
Chapter 1	What's It All About?	3
Chapter 2	Where to Get Started	7
Chapter 3	Getting Those First Cases	11
Chapter 4	The Frugal Marketeer	15
Chapter 5	The Referral Letter	23
Chapter 6	Making Your Business Hum	25
Chapter 7	PI Networks—The Key to Education and Profit	41
Chapter 8	Building the Investigative Library	43
Chapter 9	Locating People	47
Chapter 10	Manhunting—Reach Out and Touch Someone	49
Chapter 11	Searching for Hidden Information and Assets	55
Chapter 12	Tracking Down the Global Criminal	63
Chapter 13	Getting to Know You	71
Chapter 14	Investigation Simplified	73
Chapter 15	Surveillance Secrets	79
Chapter 16	Insurance Investigation	83
Chapter 17	Workman's Compensation Can Work for You	85
Chapter 18	Interview or Interrogate?	89
Chapter 19	Filling in the Gaps	93
Chapter 20	Managing Your Best Assets—Your People	97
Summary		99
Appendix	Forms and Contracts	101
Bibliography		115

Acknowledgments

The initial idea for this book was born at conferences where investigators and detectives of all types whispered their darkest secrets and deepest fears—how to get new business!

Search through the material of any investigative conference or any college or government class, and the one thing you won't see is a program teaching how to become successful in the field.

This book is written for people who want to expand their trade, as well as for those who want to leave their present job and enter the wonderful world of private investigation.

For ideas and material in this book, I would like to acknowledge the assistance of Joseph Wells, chairman of the National Association of Certified Fraud Examiners; Bill Kizorek, president of In-Photo; Ralph Thomas, president of the National Association of Investigative Specialists; and Leroy Cook of the Investigators' On-Line Network.

These individuals and many others have helped to develop and share much of the technology now used by private investigators throughout the world and have contributed greatly to our industry's body of knowledge.

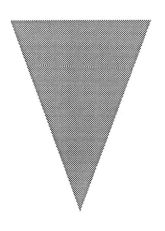

Foreword

f Ed Pankau had become a pizza maker instead of an investigator, he would own 400 pizza parlors. He would probably have the best delivery service as well, with food coming to your door carried by helicopter or snowmobile. Best yet, he would even teach his customers how to make the same pizzas in their own homes (but also sell them the fixings).

Read this book and you will see what I mean. This book is pure Pankau: Pankau the preacher, and Pankau the promoter. Ed's personality is inexorably woven into each chapter as he takes you through the world of the private investigator.

The title might have you into thinking this is a book for the beginning private investigator. It is. But it also isn't. I have been in the business for more than 30 years and was astounded at what I learned. For instance, the "Queen for a Day" interviewing technique—amazing. I tripled my personal knowledge of locating people. The sections on sources of information are so comprehensive that I have made them mandatory reading for my entire investigative staff.

The book's content is wide ranging: public records, hidden transfer of assets, searching through trash cans (especially after Valentine's Day), taking care of your staff. And it is global. Investigators in Chile will find it as useful as those in Spain, the United States, or Canada. This is another reflection of Pankau the investigator who respects no international investigative boundaries.

In fact, there are few boundaries that Ed does not cross. Don't tell him he can't do something. He'll do it just to prove it can be done. This can-do, nothing-is impossible attitude permeates the book. If you are looking for something to get you inspired enough to be a success in the investigative business, this is the book for you. Ed Pankau takes you by the hand and leads the way.

By the way, if his advice doesn't work for you, will Ed give you your money back? I can hear his voice shout out this very second, "If anyone follows the advice in this book, they are guaranteed success in the investigative business."

On a personal note, I know Ed Pankau. He is a remarkable human and a relentless promoter. As his feet hit the floor in the morning, he is probably practicing his next speech. At 7:00 that night (after a full day at the office), he is giving that speech. And at 9:00 P.M. he is taking in a Caribbean assignment from a new client who met him at the speech.

Investigations is a tough business. Rare is the private eye whose firm grows beyond a few staffers. Ed Pankau is an exception to that rule. This book is a gift to all those aspiring to build a profitable investigative business because he tells them how to do it. Just remember: he *did* it.

— Bill Kizorek
President, In-Photo

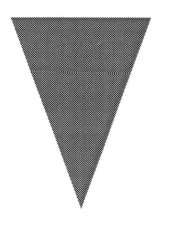

Introduction

ow would you like to be part of one of the America's fastest-growing businesses? A business with low overhead, no inventory, and a profitability directly related to your ability to do a good job? A job that is challenging, rewards creativity, and gives you the opportunity to meet with and solve the problems of people in all walks of life?

I have worked in such a business for the past 20 years and can honestly say that I enjoy it more now then when I first started. I feel the enjoyment of doing a job well and know that what I am doing everyday makes a difference in people's lives, often for their betterment. I feel positive that I have a fresh challenge in front of me: locating a missing heir, interviewing a witness, or finding the assets of someone hiding from his or her creditors.

The next person in the door may be a dreamer looking for a lost love, a business owner who's been swindled, or a little old lady who thinks the Martians are stealing her brain waves.

Who knows? But it certainly isn't boring!

If you want a new career and have the initiative to tell clients that you can make their cases or not charge them a dime, then read on, my friend. You are about to enter the wonderful world of private investigation.

What's It All About?

For all of us who have ever wanted to start our own business, the experts tell us that the easiest, least expensive, and lowest overhead businesses are to be found in the consulting field. Within the consulting field, there are many specialties: motivation, management, imaging, brokering, and a long list of others, not the least of which is the focus of this book, the private investigation business.

The private investigation industry has transformed itself in the last 10 years from a shady, snooping, gray-area business into a recognized industry of people who specialize in locating missing persons, finding hidden assets, developing cases for trial, and looking into the personal and business background of deals and dealers, whatever or wherever they may be. The private investigator has truly come out of the closet and become part of the new information age. It was the hard core of computer-wise private investigators who created much of the technology and ability to reach out and touch someone by going on-line or delving through public record filings in minutes or hours compared to the weeks or months that were the industry standard only a few years ago.

Today's private investigator has become an information specialist who relies on his telephone, computer, and fax machine far more than the surveillance car, camera, and .45 automatic that Mickey Spillane and Philip Marlowe popularized not so many years ago. In the 20 years that I have been a private investigator, I have watched this transition take place and observed our industry not only equal, but in some ways surpass, the capabilities of government investigators.

It's not unusual today, and growing as a trend, for certain areas of investigative work to be contracted out to private investigators by state, federal, and local police and regulatory agencies. The U.S. Office of Personnel Management hires contract investigators to perform

THIS BOOK WILL HELP YOU ENTER INTO THE LUCRATIVE, SHADOWY WORLD OF THE PRIVATE INVESTIGATOR.

their financial transactions. A host of other agencies including the Environmental Protection Agency, the U.S. Department of Labor, and their state counterparts are looking into the cost effectiveness of using "data detectives" to help them find the assets of people who have been fined by government agencies and refuse to pay the bill.

The U.S. Attorney's Office in the Northern District of Texas has rendered civil and criminal fines and judgments against individuals and financial institutions in excess of $50 million. Until now, less then 1 percent of the money has been collected. Once enough pressure is brought to bear by taxpayers to recover this money, some enterprising private investigator is going to make a very comfortable living collecting on these judgments for a percentage of recovery.

These same situations and circumstances exist all over the country. The government and private industry have billions of dollars tied up in uncollected judgments and unworked cases that are just begging for an enterprising investigator to get out there and hustle, cases that the government doesn't have the time, manpower, or interest to pursue, cases that will lapse in 10 years if the judgments aren't renewed and an effort isn't made to recover the money.

national security background checks. The FBI hires computer-smart investigators for record searches and contracts with industry experts to instruct its new agents in training classes. The Federal Deposit Insurance Corporation (FDIC) and Resolution Trust Corporation (RTC) are now among the largest employers of private investigators, using agencies across the country to track down hidden assets of bankers and borrowers owing billions of dollars to our failed financial institutions.

U.S. Customs and the Drug Enforcement Agency (DEA) are now learning how to use computers to find drug dealers and to trace

The beauty of the investigation business is that it doesn't require a college degree, a law enforcement certificate, or 10 years of experience in a police agency. The only criteria are the ability to do the job and enough marketing skills to develop the kinds of clients who need your services and to get them to give you a chance to show that you can do the job.

Now, I'm not saying that the college degree, the experience, and the contacts that one makes in the business don't have great value, far from it. In this business, we all live by our contacts and build on each other's strengths by networking our abilities through the associates that do our work in Boise, Omaha, or Monterey, Mexico, but the basic requirement of this business is the ability to do the job. Results count! Let me give you a few examples of people who came to this industry from outside of law enforcement and made the industry better because of their skills and experience.

Sue Rugge started her investigative career as a librarian, cataloging old records and filing away dusty books. While earning a paycheck as a librarian, she learned about the on-line flow of information and found the critical path to locating information resources all over the world. She once owned a multimillion dollar information business and sold it when it was no longer fun. Today, she operates an investigative service out of her home that is used by attorneys and corporations all over the world who want to find "all the information available" on a variety of subjects ranging from developing the medical, legal, or personal backgrounds of expert witnesses to conducting sophisticated business intelligence on their largest competitors.

The best people finders are often those who started as clerks in collection agencies and became hooked on the paper chase instead. Today, a substantial number of private investigators do nothing but locate hard-to-find defendants, witnesses, and forgotten friends for clients who pay anywhere from $100 to $1,000 per search. Probably one of the best-known people finders in the country is *George Theodore*, who spends hours on the telephone and with a computer quietly finding people, mostly for other private investigators who haven't learned all of his secret sources and don't have the time to do it themselves.

Diane Logan started as my secretary many years ago and now runs an asset searching firm with her husband, *Ken*. For Diane, it wasn't such a great step from typing reports, going to the courthouse, doing the work, and managing a staff of investigators as branch manager for my firm. Her big step was going out on her own with a little financial help from her family. Diane and Ken took the skills they learned from my firm and built a small but growing agency that anyone would be proud of. When I tried to get them back to work for me several years ago, they were far too happy to be wooed back into a business where they were not running the show.

An on-the-job injury ended *Walter Purvis'* career with the New York Police Department and forced him to look elsewhere to find a means of supporting himself and his new wife. His disability and retirement didn't quite cut the nut every month, so he started a small detective agency in Miami, specializing in criminal defense and background investigations. With his wife, Linda, working the telephone and computer, Walt has built up a nice little practice that exceeds his pay as a policeman and has given him a great deal of respect within the private investigation industry.

In sunny California, *Paul Nyland* walked out as manager of one of Pinkerton's offices and set up a records library in a warehouse furnished with a pool table and beer keg. Rather than drive downtown and wade through the courthouse records, police and private investigators alike shoot pool and maybe even drink beer at Paul's "office" while he searches through his microfiche library and finds the information that "makes their day."

These are but a few examples of the thousands of stories I hear every day from people who have found true love in the investigative industry. The one thing I find in common with all of these people is that they have become hooked on the investigative bug and the virus has spread throughout their systems and often their families'. Every one of them loves the business, works at it longer hours than they ever did at a straight job, and wouldn't trade it in for the world. When we get together at an investigators' conference, all we talk is shop. Who's got the latest marketing ideas, what's the best data base for real estate records in New England, or what's that slick little pretext to sweet-talk the utility company out of a current phone number and address?

So, I am including this caveat, warning you that you, too, may become terminally hooked into a world of modems, fax machines, data bases, and information discovery. You may well develop a terminal case of infoitis, a disease that starts by thumbing through computer magazines and investigative manuals and results in finding invoices from esoteric on-line computer services, bills that look strangely like hospital medical statements. You'll start feeling the urge to go to every investigator conference and join private investigator asso-ciations that cater to your every whim and desire for more and more information. After that, it's too late; you've become terminal, so just go right on and enjoy it.

After 20 years, I'm still alive and have just found a new strain of the disease—writing about the investigative business.

Where to Get Started

ow that you have decided to become a private investigator, the next major decision is where you are going to set up your tent? Many people wake up one morning and decide to be a private eye and then start their businesses with no more thought or planning than to operate out of their homes or apartments, right in their own communities. This may work for some, but if you truly want to be successful in this business, then it is a good idea to work where the business is. (Willie "The Actor" Sutton, when asked why he robbed banks, replied, "That's where the money is.")

This means locating in a city that has enough work to support you now and enough business (crime) to meet your growth needs if you decide to get into the PI business in a serious way. There are many ways to choose the right city or region that is conducive to the private investigator business, but if you give it a little thought, then you can double or triple your chances of success by locating yourself in an area that has a wide range of opportunities.

In working and talking with hundreds of private investigators and having opened offices in more than a few cities myself, I think I've found a formula that works most of the time. Here are a few suggestions to consider and places to look when you decide to open your business or go to work for someone while you learn the trade.

STATE CAPITALS

The capitals of each state are the repositories for the records of the secretary of state and are usually the headquarters for the majority of the state licensing and regulatory agencies and state professional associations, many of which use private investigators. The state capital is also often the largest city in the region and therefore attracts the largest businesses, banking groups, law firms, and insurance companies, which makes it a smart move to locate your agency in or near a state capital. Also, all those politicians are lawyers and love to dig up dirt on each other.

NEXUS CITIES

Look at a map of your region and you will find certain cities that are at nexus points, places where several states come together and major highways intersect. Cities like Cincinnati, Denver, Omaha, Memphis, Chicago, Philadelphia, and Baltimore are focal points for business from several states and provide easy access to a large, surrounding area from their key locations.

KEY INDUSTRIES

Certain industries have focal points in major cities that make them key centers of business activities and, therefore, a growing market for private investigators. Some of these key cities and their industries are as follows:

Financial
Boston, New York City, Atlanta, Dallas, Chicago, Kansas City, Denver, Seattle, Charlotte, Los Angeles, and San Francisco.

Insurance
Hartford, Philadelphia, Atlanta, Memphis, Minneapolis, St. Paul, San Antonio, Phoenix, and Los Angeles.

Legal
New York City, Philadelphia, Atlanta, Miami, Chicago, Dallas, Houston, Denver, St. Louis, Los Angeles, and San Francisco.

Specialized Industries
Certain cities have specific industries that bring business to private investigators because of their peculiar natures. One very good example is Las Vegas, Nevada. Many of the casinos frequently have a need to locate the assets of people who have gone over their credit limits and not paid their bills. They often hire private investigators to locate these individuals and their assets. They don't break legs or take first-born children anymore, but they will sue in court and get a judgment to seize anything that isn't nailed down.

You'd think that casinos in Las Vegas, for all their notoriety, wouldn't let a man out of the joint owing $850,000. The Hilton Las Vegas did, after verifying that he was a prince of a royal family and received more than a million dollars a month in oil revenue. They figured he'd be back the next day or the next, pay up his losses, and then go ahead and lose another couple of hundred thousand. The trouble was that the hotel managers don't understand the Mid-Eastern mind. The Saudi decided that since gambling was illegal in his religion, then Allah didn't mean for him to pay the debt, so he'd just forget about it.

As is usual in large collection cases, the hotel hired Las Vegas' biggest law firm to track the prince down and sue him for his debt (sure has changed since the old days, hasn't it). The financial statement left by the prince at the hotel indicated properties in Florida, Texas, and Oklahoma, so those were the things we tracked down first. We then searched for U.S. bank accounts and a U.S. address to serve his royal highness with lawsuit papers. After locating the properties, we contacted the realtor and found out that our prince was a football freak and had in fact not only graduated from the University of Southern California, but he still had season tickets for every game because his daughter now attended the same school. With this knowledge, it was easy enough to find his game seats from the alumni association and ticket office and serve our subject on the 50-yard line once the football season started. Once served, the prince paid his bill and we collected our fee.

Other good examples are key RTC and FDIC financial centers, such as Costa Mesa, California; Denver, Colorado; Dallas, Texas; Kansas City, Missouri; Valley Forge, Pennsylvania; Boston, Massachusetts; and Atlanta, Georgia. Each of these cities will have a world of work for years to come for investigators that are persevering enough to fill out all of those government application forms and who are sufficiently financially oriented to track down and locate the assets of borrowers, officers, and directors of failed banks and thrifts.

FOREIGN BUSINESS CENTERS

Port cities like Miami, New Orleans, Houston, San Francisco, and Seattle have unique business opportunities because they have a sea-going port and have become business centers for either the Caribbean or the Pacific Basin countries. People planning to become investigators in these or other similar cities should clearly consider expanding their knowledge, especially into marine-oriented investigations, into the countries that provide service to these ports and try to develop potential clients in these countries.

I don't mean to say that you can't start a successful private investigation in other cities, especially if you've got an uncle who is a lawyer with a firm that can keep you busy locating witnesses and serving papers, but those who have been successful in the business all agree that one of the key ingredients of their success was being located, either by design or by accident, in an area that provided a good variety of opportunities.

My own introduction into this business was purely by accident. I stopped in Houston, Texas, to visit my mother, whom I hadn't seen in over 10 years, while on my way from Miami, Florida, to a potential job in Portland, Oregon. I stopped in a little town called Tomball, Texas, on my way west and dropped in on my mother during what turned out to be the worst snowstorm in more than 50 years. Watching the snowfall, my mind told me that Oregon was not the place to be at this time of the year, so I took my mother's offer to stay for the winter and got a part-time job as a security director with a local department store while working for two private investigators on the side.

The only thing I learned from those investigators (I found their names in the yellow pages) was how *not* to do business. Each of them had his share of problems that landed him in the courthouse, taking fees and not doing the work, stringing clients along for more money, or stepping too far into the gray area, and one, the illustrious Dudley Bell, went to prison for arranging the murder of his client's common-law wife. Luckily for me, Dame Fortune smiled and dropped me right in the middle of one of the fastest-growing business regions in the United States, one with strong legal, insurance, and financial industries. It didn't hurt that Houston, in the 1970s and 1980s, was also the white-collar crime capital of the world and had every type of world-class con man and swindler alive working the streets of Houston, Austin, and Dallas, trying to separate the banks, insurance companies, and businesses from their hard-earned money. The business and bank failures that followed the spending frenzy of fraud created a growth market for both attorneys and investigators like me who worked for them.

Take a little personal advice before you take the plunge and jump into the private investigation business: try to develop as many of the above points as you can into your business plan. Your chance of success is dramatically better if you follow a plan than if you attack the business in a haphazard manner, as many of your predecessors have learned.

The $64,000 question for most people interested in getting into this business is whether they should jump into the business cold or work for someone else long enough to develop a little confidence and learn the trade. Like any other business, the more you know, the better you'll do, so it's a smart idea to work with an established investigator, see what works for him (or her), and then add your own talents and good ideas to what you learned. Several of my investigators have done this, and I wish them all well. I even send them some business every now and then when I've got a conflict or if it is in their areas of expertise.

If you work for another investigator and have a little common sense, you should learn enough about the business in a year or two to go out on your own. If you're good enough, you might make a deal with your boss to open a branch office of his existing company in a city with a new business opportunity and have the best of both worlds, using his client list and experience and your talent and ambition. You will get the benefit of your chief's experience and name identification, and he will get new business from your efforts resulting from his leads.

Getting Those First Cases

The day I decided to leave the "quacks" I was working for and start my own business, I knew I had to hit the ground running because I had only $400 in my pocket and the rent was due the next week. To survive as a private investigator, I had to find a way to get some business quickly and find a way to keep enough business to support me in my newly chosen occupation.

Everything I had ever seen, heard, or read about the private investigation business made me believe that lawyers were the very best source of business. They always needed some kind of investigative services. Therefore, I went downtown with my new, printed-that-day business cards and started working the office building commonly known as "Plaintiff's Tower." (There is one in every city—an office building, close to the courthouse, full of hungry, young lawyers.)

I started at the top floor and talked to every lawyer who would give me five minutes of his time. I wanted to be different from all the other investigators who were already established in town, so I made each attorney an offer that has come to be my trademark in the industry and has worked on almost every client that has ever allowed me in his door. I asked each of them to give me their worst, nastiest, toughest case, the one that no one else could solve, and that I would do it right, or they didn't owe me a dime. Whether it was locating a witness, finding the address of a debtor, or following some errant spouse, I wanted to show them what I could do and that I could do it as well or better than the investigator they normally used.

By using this approach, I quickly found that many of the lawyers had cases that had been worked unsuccessfully by other investigators. These cases were now moldering in the corners of some junior associate lawyer's office because they couldn't put the pieces of the puzzle together. By offering a deal that they can't refuse, most lawyers will give you a chance.

I tried this approach on my first prospective client, who listened for five minutes and then sent me after his client, a prostitute who had fallen in a grocery store and was now the prospective recipient of a $20,000 insurance settlement, if her lawyer could find her. The problem was that Maria had moved frequently since hiring her lawyer two years before. It seems that law school hadn't taught my new client how to find prostitutes, and she was smart enough not to get arrested, which foiled the efforts of the previous investigators the lawyer hired, who were ex-policemen. So I got a chance to show my stuff.

I went out to Maria's neighborhood that night and knocked on the door at her last address, hoping to find someone who knew something about her. After nobody appeared at the door, I saw several young studs playing basketball at the neighborhood community center and asked them if they could tell me about Maria or where she was now staying. To more fully get the attention of these neighborhood sources, I pulled out a $20 bill and my favorite gravity knife, cut the $20 in half, and handed one of two halves to the most promising looking of these pimply-faced boys. Now that I had his immediate attention, I explained that Maria had recently come into some money and that he would get not only the other half of my $20, but at least another $20 from Maria, once I could find her and tell her where to meet me to collect her new pot of gold.

My little informants chatted between themselves in Spanish for a few minutes and then took me to the nearest pay phone, hit me up for a quarter, and dialed Maria's number. Once I had her on the line, it was easy enough to explain to Maria that this sweet young lawyer she'd hired had won her a juicy settlement and that he just needed her to come sign the papers and pick up her money. Maria called me all kinds of wonderful and told me where to meet her the next morning. She offered to see me that night at the bar she was working, but I felt that I had enough luck for one day and that if I pushed it any further, I probably would get my initials carved in my chest at the

kind of club that Maria was dancing in. (Besides, I had made a date with the secretary of my new-found lawyer client and wanted a chance to impress her before I gave the good news to her boss.)

The next morning, 9 A.M. bright and shiny, I picked up Maria in her Sunday-best go-to-church clothes and took her to her lawyer's office. Maria smiled, the lawyer smiled, and when the checks were cut, I smiled too. The lawyer gave me a funny look and asked, "Ed, how the hell did you find her? I have looked for her for three years with a couple of police investigators and haven't even come close."

I grinned back and said, "Friend, you told me to find her, not to tell you how! That information costs extra!" I picked up my check and took Maria home. To this day, that lawyer still hasn't figured it out, but he is still a great client.

The moral of the story is that lawyers are one of the best sources of new or day-to-day business for any private investigator. Every lawyer represents dozens of clients and has some dog-eared old file sitting on his desk, just waiting for you to come and make him an offer he can't refuse. Try it—I bet that it works for you too.

The day after I found Maria I got another case from a lawyer in that same building, and a third case the next day. On Friday I got my first referral, from my first client who, while having lunch with another lawyer, told him about the prostitute I had found when no one else could. This new lawyer got my name and phone number from my first client, and told me that he had to locate and serve nine witnesses for trial Monday morning. (I found out later that this is a very common problem. Lawyers always wait until the last minute to find their witnesses then rush to a private investigator because no sheriff or constable can or will do that kind of job, locating and serving witnesses, over a weekend).

Fortunately for me, the courthouse was not closed yet, so I found current addresses on six of the nine witnesses by peeking at voter registration, marriage, and property tax records. That weekend, while out serving the six witnesses I had located, I got enough information from two of them who had worked with three of the others that I was able to find and serve eight of the nine witnesses by Monday morning. The ninth witness, finding a note and a copy of my subpoena on his door, called the lawyer Monday morning and kept me batting 1,000.

All added up, I made over $1,000 that week by locating the prostitute, an insurance company defendant, and the nine witnesses. This was more money than I had ever made as a federal agent and looked damned good, especially in 1973, when a dollar was really a dollar. It was beginning to look like I might have a career, or at least a job for a while, as a private investigator.

If you want to be successful in any business, you must be innovative and recognize new ideas and opportunities as they arise. Opportunities are all around, bringing new kinds of clients and new kinds of work. The best rules I learned while getting started still apply today. Creativity is the key! To achieve success, be different from your competition and listen to your clients. Ask the following questions and you will establish your client's needs and budget every time:

1. What kind of case do you have?
2. What is your ultimate goal from my investigation?
3. What initial budget should we establish in this case?

By the time you have your client to this point, the case is yours. The client has committed his case to you and now only wants results. The best way to show results is to devise, with your client, an investigative plan of action detailing the steps and phases of your case, with a cost per phase conducted. Through meeting with your client and understanding his goal, you have educated and impressed upon him your abilities and given him an expectation of what he will get and when it will be done. This is the best selling tool in the business.

Always ask your client what kind of budget he has in mind when hiring you. Very often, say 60 percent or more of the time, your client expects to pay more than you think it will cost, in which case you can be a hero by coming in under his budget and beating his expectations. If he has a much lower figure in mind, then you have to educate him about what it costs to do the job, or you can agree to start the case within his budget, calling this Phase I, a preliminary step for further investigations. You will get more business and have far less trouble getting paid when your client knows and agrees up front to what you're going to do. (It always helps to reinforce this in writing, too.)

The next step, after you have been hired, is to fax or mail your client a contract confirming your agreement. This smart little step makes sure you get paid by the few flaky clients that you're going to pick up along the way. Having a signed contract helps you to avoid legal costs in suing clients or, as most investigators do, kissing a percentage of their fees good-bye at the end of every year on their financial statements.

CHAPTER 4

The Frugal Marketeer

Every time experienced investigators see a full-page ad in the yellow pages or trade magazines announcing the services of a new investigative or security agency, we shake our heads. If 20 years of experience has taught us anything, it's that this type of advertising is the least cost-effective and most expensive means to get new business, and almost never results in the kind of quality business we all hope to build.

Pick up the local yellow pages sometime and call the telephone numbers listed in the biggest ads. If the phone book has been in service for more than six months, you'll find that half of the big advertising telephone numbers are disconnected or not in service. This alone should tell you that the ads didn't bring in enough business to justify their existence and that the price of these ads probably sped up their purchasers' business downfall.

At every investigators conference, one of the most talked-about subjects, whispered in the dark corners of bars and meeting rooms, is about what kind of advertising works and what strategies and tactics bring in new business and new clients. You see, many detectives have very good investigative skills, honed by many years in law enforcement or private practice, but very few of them have any experience in or have taken courses in marketing, management, or finance, the subjects that teach them how to make their businesses hum. They've never been taught that you can be the best investigator in the world but go dead broke in a year if clients don't know you're out there and you fail to develop an expanding list of clients who use your services and become your future cheerleaders.

Many aspiring private investigators often ask what courses to take in college to help them learn the business and develop their skills so that they can open their own agencies someday. When asked for advice, I stress that every future investigator should take at least one business course per semester so he or she can develop a good business background, as well as learn how to be a better investigator. If you're going to understand a criminal case or investigate a criminal, you've got to understand his *modus operandi*. To investigate a businessman, you must first understand business and learn the things that your subject has to have done in the business world to perpetrate his or her crime.

What is the best means of developing new business through advertising and marketing? Well, I thought you'd never ask. Here's a list of things that have worked for many of the most successful investigators in the country.

BAR ASSOCIATION JOURNALS AND MAGAZINES

Almost every county and every state have a bar journal that is the association magazine of its constituent attorneys. Many of these magazines, in addition to publishing the viewpoints and opinions of their local attorneys, accept advertising from outside vendors, such as investigators, consultants, and suppliers of goods and services that lawyers everywhere use. These journals, which are mailed free each month (or bimonthly or quarterly), are among the few publications that every lawyer reads.

Some lawyers read them for the articles; others look to see which attorneys were hired on new cases, which ones have been chastised by the bar association grievance committee, or which ones made their final listing in the obituaries. For whatever reason, they all look at these magazines (maybe because they're free)

MY FIRM, INTERTECT, OFTEN ADVERTISES IN LEGAL JOURNALS. THIS AD RAN IN *THE HOUSTON LAWYER*.

and will notice your ad if it stands out from the rest or challenges them to make a decision.

After experimenting with numerous ads, the one I like best has a photo of my smiling face and big bold letters **"Do you know this man?"** at the top right-hand side of the page. (When you advertise, always ask that your ad be placed on the right-hand side of the page because it is twice as visible as a left-side page ad.) Advertising gurus have determined that people will almost always stop reading to answer a question, so I tried it in an ad. Feedback from my clients told me that this ad stood out from all the others in the book, and, better yet, they remembered it!

INVESTIGATOR MAGAZINES AND NEWSLETTERS

Marketing to other investigators is very often a frustrating and futile business. Most investigators think they can do the work themselves (and probably can), and few, if any, want to hear or read about someone else's success when they are trying to build a business of their own.

One of the exceptions to this rule is when an investigative agency has a unique product or provides a service in a very defined specialty or marketplace where there is little or no competition. An example of this is the investigator who advertises his or her specialty in electronic countermeasures or area specialists with capabilities in Eastern Europe, the Middle East, or Latin America. These investigators often benefit from such advertising because they fill a need that other investigators are unable to fulfill in their own practice but often require to provide a full range of services to their clients.

One marketing idea that you should always consider in your trade newsletters and journals is sending out public announcements of any expansion to new offices, acquisition of new skills, and awards granted to your agency and its investigators. This will alert members to your new circumstances and capabilities and remind them of your name when they have need of the types of services you provide. Since these announcements are published gratuitously for its members, this is also a very cost-effective means of keeping your name in the news. (It doesn't get much cheaper than free!)

CLIENT NEWSLETTERS

As you develop in your business and assist your clients in bigger and better deals, you should consider their own newspapers and journals as a vehicle to spread your name throughout their firm. Through the wonders of modern technology—specifically the word processor and graphics software available to every company—almost every business produces its own in-house publication to congratulate company employees and educate the staff on new policies and procedures.

When a client of this type hires you to do an investigation, talk with your client and his or her publication director about publicizing the facts and circumstances of your investigation so that all the company employees (and often their vendors, who are also on the mailing lists) can benefit from their new lessons. (It may be necessary or advisable to change the names of the subjects, but you can run this by the legal department.)

An article of this type reinforces the company's commitment to internal security and recognizes your firm, to one and all, as an integral part of its team. Through this medium, the company now becomes your cheerleader and officially blesses your work and your relationship with the company.

Whatever type of advertising you do, develop at least two or three different ads of varying sizes and wording so that your clients don't become visually accustomed to your same ad time after time. If they see the same ad every month, it becomes invisible because their eyes immediately recognize the familiar ad and go on to something else. If you can't afford to be in every issue of the magazine or journal, consider advertising in every other issue. The people who read the magazine regularly will still see you there on a frequent basis and recognize your continuing ad, but you have just cut your advertising costs in half.

CLIENT TRADE JOURNALS

If the majority of your clients are in a specific industry, or if you wish to develop clients in a certain association or group, then you need to find their written mouthpiece. This is usually a newsletter or trade journal that may range from several photocopied sheets to a professionally done 80-page magazine that promotes the association to its readership.

Just like a bar journal, this magazine is read primarily by its association members, but these magazines are almost always looking for articles of interest to its members and sell just enough advertising to pay for publication costs. Here is where you can use your investigative skills and share your knowledge with potential clients by writing an article that will pique their interest.

For more than several years, I've been writing for several trade journals to help new investigators learn the business and share a few of my secrets with other professionals in return for their interest. Now, this isn't done just out of the goodness of my heart. You see, I've found this is the true marketing road to success because people tear out and save those articles they find of value and call the writer whenever they need someone in that area of expertise. Those full-page, high-dollar ads will still be in the magazine when it hits the trash can or is put up on the shelf along with the other old magazines, but a good article is often torn out and kept in the investigative library and referred to frequently. (I've had more than 200 requests for reprints of "Tracking the Global Criminal," an excerpt from this book that was published earlier in *Security Management* magazine.)

Widows BEWARE

After twenty or thirty years of hard work, you are now a successful business executive or owner. You have paid your dues, built your family's future with sweat, blood and tears, and feel a well-deserved security in knowing that you and your family have the money to retire, or in a worst case scenario, provide for their protection in the case of your death.

Sounds morbid, doesn't it, sort of grizzly. Why should you ever think about something like that? You have another twenty years. You are bullet proof and invisible (or so you think). But what about your spouse? What would happen to him or her if you were suddenly gone? Does he or she have the emotional support, so necessary from friends and family to help through the process of your death and the readjustment of carrying on daily life. If not, chances are he or she could become a victim of the professional con.

This con is the kind that peruses obituaries, newspapers and divorce settlements in court records to target affluent people in their weakest moments. They target their prey in the paper and follow them, literally or figuratively, until they find the magic moment to "meet" by accident.

Jane was the wife of the owner of a successful upstate brewing business. Her husband of 16 years, Frank, was successful by all standards, both in his business and as a respected member of the community.

When Frank died, Jane threw herself into her work, frantically attempting to lose herself so that she wouldn't have to think of the life she had lost. Then, one day after she had been featured in a local newspaper as woman business owner of the year, Jane went to a local fundraiser where she met a man who she thought was the gentleman of her dreams. Little did she know that her dreams would turn into her worst nightmare.

Doctor Vannerson was a retired physician who now spent his time managing investments. He had all the social graces, the looks of Marcus Welby, and a soft professional voice that made Jane hang on his every word. His charm, confidence and sincere understanding instantly put Jane at ease

---

I REGULARLY WRITE COLUMNS FOR ASSOCIATIONS WHOSE MEMBERS OFTEN HAVE NEED OF PRIVATE INVESTIGATORS. THIS FRAUD COLUMN, "WIDOWS BEWARE," RAN IN *DBA: HOUSTON'S BUSINESS SOURCE*.

If you can't come up with a good idea for an article, ask your reader some pertinent questions or give him a test. One of the few ads produced within our industry that I liked was a short, 10-question test that quizzed the reader on his knowledge of drug screening. It forced me to think and made me wonder if I should set up the same procedures to protect my company and employees from the rotten apples that sold drugs and stole to support their personal habits. If it worked on me, it sure would work on a corporate client!

BROCHURES

Your brochure is an essential part of your company's promotion and should answer several key questions for someone considering your services. The first key questions are "What's in it for me? Why should I use your services instead of someone else, and how will it help me in my business."

To answer these questions in your bro-chure, you must describe the services that you provide and the benefits they can bring to the client. The key selling points of a brochure are the value of your service and the benefits that are derived from its use. Your brochure must convey your company's ability and communicate the message that you want to send.

Rather than trying to be all things to all people, you should sell your strengths rather than dilute yourself through advertising a dozen different services. If you have several special skills or have built a firm that has expertise in several areas, then I would recommend that you produce a separate small brochure on each area of expertise and send those brochures to the focused clients who use those services.

Perhaps the question most often asked about brochures is the size and cost of developing and printing. Through a lot of trial and error, and looking at the brochures of hundreds of other investigators, I have come to the

SAFETY, SECURITY & INVESTIGATION PROFESSIONALS

A firm of professional, experienced, certified experts available for consultation or examination of cases requiring expert opinions or testimony.

Edmund J. Pankau, C.L.I., C.F.E., C.P.P.
Expertise:
Financial Fraud Examination
Investigator Industry Standards
Hidden Asset Location

Frank W. Robinson, C.F.E., C.P.P.
Expertise:
Building Safety and Security
Fire Prevention Procedures
Security Negligence Issues

Allan R. Wick, C.F.E., C.P.P.
Expertise:
Electronic Counter Measures
Security Planning Procedures
Premesis Liability Examination

INTERTECT
THE INTEGRITY OF YOUR BUSINESS... IS OUR BUSINESS

Expert Witness Testimony
Pre-Trial Investigation
Legal & Medical Malpractice Examination
Intellectual Property & Trademark Fraud
Discovery of Undisclosed Assets
Security & Safety Planning
Life, Health, Injury Examination

5300 Memorial Drive, Suite 450 • Houston, Texas 77007

713-880-1111

Houston • Dallas • San Antonio • Beaumont • Corpus Christi • Austin • Atlanta • Phoenix   License C-1249

conclusion that any growth-oriented investigative agency should have two brochures:

1. An inexpensive, cost-effective fold-over brochure that fits in a legal size envelope
2. A larger, more comprehensive, quality brochure to give clients in formal presentations and proposals

The small brochure should list the services you provide and feature one or two key points about your expertise or your company principals. This brochure, which should cost between 15 and 30 cents a copy, should be used as an introduction of your services as a means for people to contact you for more information. Because of its low cost, you can feel comfortable in sending out 100 or more brochures each month to a targeted group of potential clients and expect a good return on your investment.

The larger brochure, which I recommend you deliver in person, should be a corporate-level brochure that describes your various services, the principals of your firm, and your corporate message. This brochure is meant to inspire confidence in your firm and reinforce the reason why the client contacted you in the first place. Looking at other investigators' brochures, I've noticed that they spend anywhere from $1 to $10 and more on these deluxe presentation brochures.

Through talking to clients, I have learned that a 10- or 20-page brochure does no better than a smaller, well-thought-out, well-produced brochure that answers a prospective client's questions. I prefer a heavy paper brochure with a pocket on the back flap that can hold additional articles and your business card. This kind of brochure gives you the flexibility to add different materials inside the presentation folder and change the address of your brochure just by changing your business card. Too many investigators invest in brochures and then six months or a year later they change addresses, personnel, or their marketing focus, forcing them to either design a new brochure or stick with their old ways.

COMPANY NEWSLETTERS

For several years, I've been examining other industry's newsletters and have been thinking about developing one for my own firm. A company newsletter, printed quarterly, is inexpensive, informative, and enhances your company's visibility with existing and new clients. By featuring your expertise in recent cases and reprinting articles of interest to your client base, the company newsletter can act as an excellent supplement to your brochure and remind clients of your availability and expertise.

PROFESSIONAL PRESENTATIONS

Most investigators don't realize it, but they are in the business most people dream of. Nearly everyone thinks that he or she would be a great investigator and could do every bit as good as Colombo or Rockford, if only given a chance. These people—most of them trapped in everyday jobs—would love to hear about your business. They take vicarious pleasure in hearing how you solved a whodunit.

On the local level, they'll buy your breakfast, and if they really like you, they'll pay you up to $1,000 or more a day just to hear you tell them how much they really need your services. If you don't think this could be true, my speaking fees alone came to almost $50,000 last year, talking to accountants, auditors, investigators, and others who just have the fantasy of being an investigator. (If someone had told me this several years ago, I wouldn't have believed them either.)

The best way to get started is with your local civic and professional associations. Where do you find them? Just look on the business page of your local newspaper or in the meetings column of your local business journal for the listing of associations, when and where they meet, and if they have a speaker.

The first time I spoke at such a meeting, I didn't know what to say, so I asked them what they wanted to know. Most of the people wanted to know how to get into the investigations business, what was my most difficult case, and if this business was really dangerous. Those questions I could answer. The rest of my presentation developed, step by step, getting a little more polished and confident at each additional talk.

If you find you like speaking and want to develop your skills into a profession, then I would highly recommend your local Toastmaster or a local chapter of the National Speaker's Association. These associations specialize in developing your speaking skills and teaching you how to market those skills into a profession. (If you can't find a local chapter, then contact the NSA headquarters at 3877 N. 7th Street, Suite 350, Phoenix, AZ 85014.)

PUT IT IN WRITING

The spoken word is a beautiful thing, but once given (unless it's recorded), it's gone. If you really want a larger audience and a way to preserve your ideas forever, they've got to be in print.

SEARCH FOR ASSETS — A private investigator was instrumental in developing leads to uncover possible hidden assets of deposed former Panamanian leader Gen. Antonio Noriega, who is shown in this 1990 U.S. Marshal booking shot. Ed Pankau found a computer printout listing more than $800 million in assets held in 18 countries, assets he is convinced are Noriega's personal holdings.

VARIOUS NEWSPAPER CLIPPINGS IN NATIONAL PUBLICATIONS THAT HAVE FEATURED ARTICLES ON THE AUTHOR. EXPOSURE LIKE THIS USUALLY PAYS OFF IN NEW ASSIGNMENTS.

The Referral Letter

Every sales manual I've ever read preached the gospel of positive reinforcement. People like to be stroked and like to know that you appreciate them. Whenever a new client calls, ask him or her how he or she was referred to you.

If sent by a friend, attorney, or former client, the best thing you can do is to shoot out an atta-boy letter thanking him for being your cheerleader. (If you tell 10 people you are the greatest detective in the world, one or two will buy your story, but if they hear it from someone else, someone who saw it with his own eyes, nine out of 10 will bite and use your services.)

By thanking them with a personal note, you can make everyone you know one of your cheerleaders just by showing them that you value their praise. Send them a short note of appreciation and they will refer business to you again and again. Just load a short thank you note like the following in your word processor and your secretary can send it out without your blinking an eye.

DATE

(NAME)
(TITLE)
(COMPANY)
(ADDRESS)
(CITY, STATE, ZIP)

RE: A personal thank you for the referral

Dear (CLIENT):
I would like to extend a personal thank you for your recent referral of [NAME] of [COMPANY] to our firm. Your professional courtesy and consideration in our behalf represent the greatest compliment we can be paid. It is with much pride that I am worthy of your trust. In appreciation, I remain,

Respectfully,

(YOUR SIGNATURE)

Making Your Business Hum

he computer, and the information that it brings to our fingertips, is one of the greatest investigative tools developed in the twentieth century. Through the wonders of microchip technology, we can now search a multitude of data bases and analyze millions of information items relevant to our investigations. The computer itself does not conduct investigations; that is still, and will remain, the investigator's domain. What the computer does is to narrow the parameters of the search and focus the investigation far faster than any means previously available. The computer allows us to network with other resources and agencies across the globe and provides an instantaneous transmission of data that can outrun even the fastest criminal.

The computer itself is just the visual box, a television screen that portrays the information from its data bases. These data bases and the information stored in their files are the true treasure trove of information. These data bases can be classified in many ways, based on the type of information they provide. The following are seven categories that most investigators find useful in their trade:

1. Law Enforcement/Intelligence
2. Insurance Industry Data Bases
3. Public Record Filings
4. Credit Reports
5. Communication/Media
6. Scientific/Technical
7. People/Money

Within each of these categories, you will find a wide range of resources. These resources serve a specific purpose, but all contribute to the investigator's body of knowledge and add to the ability to investigate various aspects of crime.

LAW ENFORCEMENT/INTELLIGENCE

For many years, law enforcement agencies have collected criminal history information and other statistics that help identify criminals, determine their whereabouts, and provide intelligence on members associated with criminal acts such as organized crime families, theft rings, and serial criminals. In recent years, new data bases have been developed to provide financial information and "modus operandi" information to help law enforcement officers identify patterns of crimes in the hope of recognizing acts perpetrated nationwide by serial criminals.

• National Crime Information Center. The NCIC was developed as a tool for local law enforcement agencies to access criminal history information nationwide. The FBI organized, built, and maintains this data base and collects criminal arrest, conviction, and intelligence information on wanted suspects, both in the United States and abroad. The FBI also maintains two other data bases, the National Stolen Property Index (NSPI) (which includes stolen government and military property) and the National Fraudulent Index (NFI).

• INTERPOL. The International Criminal Police Organization, better known as INTERPOL, is a network of national, central police bureaus in more than 155 member countries that share information with each other to assist law enforcement agencies in the detection and deterrence of international crime. Each bureau is an agency of that member country's government and serves as the liaison between that law enforcement agency and the INTERPOL network. The types of crimes and investigations that INTERPOL can provide information on include the following:
   —Location of suspects, fugitives, and witnesses
   —Criminal history checks
   —Prevention of terrorism

   —Stolen artwork
   —Tracing of weapons
   —Tracing motor vehicles, license plates, and driver's checks

• El Paso Intelligence Center (EPIC). EPIC is a proprietary data base of U.S. Customs to assist this agency in documenting the foreign travel and return of individuals reentering the United States from a foreign port. This data base is extremely helpful in identifying people who make frequent trips outside of the United States and has led to the identification and arrest of thousands of people involved in the theft, smuggling, and drug trade. (EPIC is discussed further in Chapter 12.)

• Financial Crime Enforcement Network, 3833 N. Fairfax Drive, Arlington, VA 22203 (FinCen). FinCen was developed as a division of the U.S. Treasury Department to provide public record information, financial analysis, and other computerized data on drug dealers and other high-dollar money launderers and white-collar criminals. This data base is maintained by the U.S. Treasury and is used by local, state, and federal law enforcement agencies and regulatory agencies to determine financial activities and locate assets in cases where white-collar criminals are suspected of financial fraud. Some data bases searched by FinCen include the following:
   —Cash Transaction Reports (CTRs). Provide information on individuals conducting financial transactions of $10,000 or more. Initially required of banks and financial institutions, this reporting requirement is now required of title companies, auto dealers, and others receiving cash funds in excess of $10,000.
   —EPIC.
   —Real Property. FinCen searches the data bases of public record providers to identify both tax assessment and real property ownership of targets of investigation and related parties. Investigations indicate that the majority of white-collar criminals frequently hide real property in their spouses' maiden names. Where investigators once had to search real

property ownership by township or county records, computerized resources have combined this information so that searches can be conducted by state, region, or almost nationally (some states are not yet computerized and easily accessible) to identify real property ownership or taxation and ownership on a much larger scale.

—Publications. Using communication data bases, FinCen searches for newspaper, magazine, and other publication records of target individuals and their related business entities to identify their current location and activities. These searches will often lead to a new business location and financial activities of white collar criminals by reporting their stock transactions, purchases, sales or other business activities reported by local and national publications.

—Intelligence. FinCen collates the information of many data bases to search for patterns of financial criminals that will help identify new targets and provide clues to their current activities. By combining information on the foreign travel, registration of new business entities, location of cash transactions, and large financial purchases, this analysis can often identify parties not discovered through traditional investigative means and trace the source of funds back to illegal enterprises.

• Federal Aviation Administration (FAA). FAA maintains records reflecting the chain of ownership of all civil aircraft in the United States. These records include documents pertaining to the manufacture, sale, transfer, inspection, and modification of aircraft, including the bill of sale, contracts, mortgages, and liens.

The FAA also maintains records on pilots, aircraft mechanics, flight engineers, and others whom it certifies in flight safety positions. (If you ever want to locate a pilot, call the FAA and ask where his next physical is going to be held. One of its representatives can tell you in advance where he will be and give you the means to establish a meaningful relationship at his next physical.)

• Social Security Administration. This agency, within the Department of Health and Human Services, maintains the original applications for Social Security numbers that include date of birth, place of birth, sex, race, and parents' names and address at the time of application. The first three digits of a Social Security number indicate its assigned area of issuance. This is one of the best tools to determine where a person grew up and often gives another place to investigate for assets, by identifying the area that many people either run home to or where their parents have lived and died and remembered them in their wills.

• U.S. Coast Guard. This agency maintains the names of merchant mariners on U.S. vessels and any investigative records pertaining to them. The Coast Guard also provides records on documented U.S. vessels that includes most boats over 40 tons registered in this country. When searching for a yacht, the U.S. Coast Guard Marine Inspection Office should be high on your list.

INSURANCE INDUSTRY DATA BASES

Aside from law enforcement, many industries create their own intelligence data bases to help spot emerging trends and individuals who cause frequent financial losses to their industries.

Many of the nation's leading insurance companies contribute claim information to computer bureaus that collate and merge the information to identify frequent claimants and locations of claims (one of the ways insurers identify crime rings is by determining the existence of frequent or multiple claims at a single location). This search pattern defeats the use of multiple names and the use of third parties in claim fraud by identifying and examining frequent claim addresses to determine the true owner or users of the address and comparing them against claim files.

• American Insurance Services Group, 700 New Brunswick Avenue, Rahway, NJ. As recently as several years ago, there were eight index bureaus scattered around the country that all

APPLICATION FOR CERTIFICATION OF BIRTH

INSTRUCTIONS	COPIES REQUESTED	DO NOT WRITE IN THIS SPACE
THE FEE FOR EACH CERTIFICATION MUST BE SUBMITTED WITH THIS APPLICATION. REMITTANCES MUST BE MADE PAYABLE TO THE TEXAS DEPARTMENT OF HEALTH. MAIL THIS APPLICATION TO BUREAU OF VITAL STATISTICS Texas Department of Health 1100 West 49th St. Austin, Texas 78756-3191	CERTIFICATION OF BIRTH $8.00* (HOW MANY) / CERTIFICATION OF BIRTH (Wallet-size) $8.00 (HOW MANY) / TOTAL AMOUNT ENCLOSED: $	REQUEST NO. AND DATE / AMOUNT / CODE

WARNING: The penalty for knowingly making a false statement in this form can be 2-10 years in prison and a fine of up to $5,000. (Vernon's Texas Health and Safety Code, Chapter 195)

INFORMATION ABOUT PERSON WHOSE BIRTH CERTIFICATE IS REQUESTED (TYPE OR PRINT)

	FIRST NAME	MIDDLE NAME	LAST NAME
1. FULL NAME OF PERSON	Jane	Ann	Williams

2. DATE OF BIRTH	MONTH December	DAY 1	YEAR 1990	3. SEX Female

4. PLACE OF BIRTH	CITY OR TOWN Houston	COUNTY Harris	STATE Texas

5. FULL NAME OF FATHER	FIRST NAME John	MIDDLE NAME Michael	LAST NAME Williams

6. FULL MAIDEN NAME OF MOTHER	FIRST NAME Mary	MIDDLE NAME Carol	LAST NAME (MAIDEN) Williams

PERSON REQUESTING CERTIFICATION OF BIRTH

7. DO YOU WANT THE NAMES OF THE PARENTS SHOWN ON THE CERTIFICATION OF BIRTH? YES ☒ NO ☐

8. PURPOSE FOR WHICH CERTIFICATION OF BIRTH IS TO BE USED

9. RELATIONSHIP TO PERSON NAMED IN ITEM 1 ABOVE (Self, Mother, Attorney, Employer, Etc.) Mother

10. SIGNATURE OF APPLICANT

11. TELEPHONE (8 a.m. to 5 p.m.) (713) 944-1234

12. ADDRESS OF APPLICANT (Type or Print)	STREET ADDRESS 567 8th Street	13. Date Signed 03/27/91
	CITY OR TOWN Houston	STATE TX	ZIP CODE 77057

IF YOU WANT THE CERTIFICATION OF BIRTH MAILED TO SOME OTHER PERSON, COMPLETE THIS SECTION

TYPE OR PRINT
NAME
STREET ADDRESS
CITY OR TOWN | STATE | ZIP CODE

VS-141, REV. 9/89

PLEASE COMPLETE AND RETURN

*THE FEE FOR EACH CERTIFICATION OF BIRTH IS $8.00 REGARDLESS OF SIZE.

NOTE: The searching fee is non-refundable nor transferable when a record is not located.

** A CERTIFICATION OF BIRTH (WALLET SIZE) INCLUDES ONLY THE INFORMATION SHOWN IN THE SAMPLE AT RIGHT.

TEXAS DEPARTMENT OF HEALTH
BUREAU OF VITAL STATISTICS
FILE NO. 100343-57
NAME John Henry Doe
DATE OF BIRTH 5-5-57 SEX Male
PLACE OF BIRTH Austin, Texas
DATE FILED 6-6-57 DATE ISSUED 1-5-79
This is a true certification of name and birth facts as recorded in this office. Issued under authority of Rule 34a, Article 4477, Revised Civil Statutes of Texas.
W D CARROLL, STATE REGISTRAR
CERTIFICATION OF BIRTH
ACTUAL SIZE 2½" X 3¾"

BIRTH CERTIFICATES ARE AMONG THE FIRST PUBLIC DOCUMENT INVESTIGATORS SEARCH FOR TO GAIN INFORMATION ABOUT A SUBJECT.

searched claim information manually to identify potential fraud. Through the advent of the computer and the need for national claims information, these index bureaus have merged into a central operation directed by American Insurance Services Group. This company owns and manages two data bases, the Central Index Bureau (CIB) and the Property Insurance Loss Register (PILR) that helps law enforcement and insurance agencies identify the history of claimants, the number of claims by an individual, the number of claims at a given address, and possible patterns of fraud.

• National Insurance Crime Bureau, 10330 S. Roberts Road, 3A, Palos Hills, IL 60456. This agency combines the investiga-

tive and data gathering activities of the National Automobile Theft Bureau and the Insurance Crime Prevention Institute and collects data from law enforcement agencies and insurance companies concerning insurance claim fraud and auto theft.

PUBLIC RECORD FILINGS

Every city, county, state, and federal jurisdiction maintains records of the activities of their agencies and the people who act within their systems. These public records are the largest data base of information in the United States and provide information on literally everyone in the country, far exceeding most records accessed by law enforcement agencies, which only maintain records on one out of every five individuals who have been involved in criminal activities. The public records provide a history of the personal, business, litigation, and financial activities of citizens and noncitizens alike, all of whom must register their deeds and activities through these public records systems.

The public record system maintains records in four primary areas that are of assistance to the investigator:

1. *Personal Identification and Location.* Records such as voter registration, marriage license, and driver's license registrations can often provide full legal names, current and prior addresses, dates of birth, and Social Security numbers of individuals who file for or obtain these documents. These records are easily obtainable through county or state agencies and provide the fastest and most cost effective means of locating individuals or identifying their current or former addresses (the first three numbers of the Social Security number identify the area in which the individ-

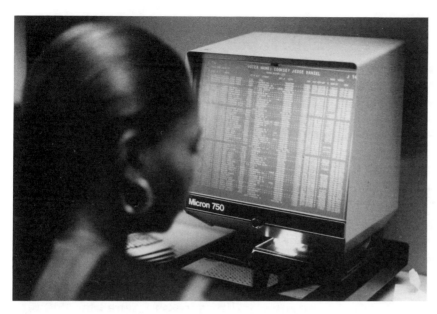

A COMPUTER AND THE RIGHT NETWORKS CAN BRING VOTER REGISTRATION AND OTHER PUBLIC RECORDS RIGHT INTO YOUR OFFICE.

an extensive data base, as almost every individual in this country is either a plaintiff, defendant, or witness in civil case litigation sometime in his or her life. The types of cases that encompass civil litigation include actions for divorce, nonpayment of debt, breach of contract, loan default, injury claims, and disputes over many real or imagined wrongs. Both the civil and criminal records of lawsuits in litigation are public records, freely available to any interested party.

Every investigator should become familiar with the criminal and civil courthouses and the records they contain because these records often provide detailed information that is invaluable in developing background information on their subjects. Levels of courts include municipal, county, district/superior, federal, and criminal/civil/bankruptcy.

4. *Asset Ownership.* To own or control property in this country, the purchaser of this property must fill out a long list of documents that provides a clear trail for the financial investigator.

From the purchase of the property (often conducted at a title company) to the payment of taxes through the county tax assessor and the filing of the real property deed at the county recorder's office, each step provides the investigator with a document that details the date, financial parameters, and parties involved in the transaction.

The tax assessor and the county recorder records are now computerized in many states and can quickly be accessed through a data base that will provide the identification of counties in which the party owns or pays taxes on property. This resource provides the investigator with the location to obtain the documents and records that detail the property transaction's full history.

Another record, often overlooked by financial investigators, is the county probate record, the document source that details the assets and liabilities of parties through the distribution of

ual was issued a Social Security registration. This information provides investigators with a means to determine where an individual was either born, grew up, or first entered the United States in many cases).

2. *Business Affiliations.* Records of the secretary of state corporate division, county assumed name filings, and uniform commercial code (UCC) records provide the names of people registering business entities, the identity of businesses registered by individuals, or other companies and reveal the names and addresses of financial institutions and other creditors that conducted financial transactions with a party obtaining credit or financing. UCC records also provide a documentation of collateral for loans that will identify and locate the existence of those assets.

3. *Litigation.* The data bases of names of people involved in lawsuits, both criminal and civil, provide valuable information to the investigator seeking former associates, witnesses, or third parties with knowledge of the activities of investigation targets.

The searching of these litigation records is frequently described as "sniffing out the vintage where the sour grapes are stored," as it provides a detailed list of the people who have personal, business, and financial grudges against the subject of the investigation. These records provide their estate. In those cases where inheritance is an issue in establishing someone's true net worth, the probate records are often the best resource to determine the extent of assets and liabilities of a person at the time of their death and the partitioning of the estate to the heirs.

Where investigators frequently spent hours pouring over huge, hand-written volumes in courthouses, public information resellers like Prentice Hall On-Line have made a new industry of computerizing and collating these public record transactions. These companies, and other public record resellers, have accumulated the rights to resell these millions of records that provide valuable insight into the activities that constitute our daily lives.

• Information America (IA), 600 W. Peachtree St., N.W., Ste. 1200, Atlanta, GA 30308. This is a nationwide retrieval service that collects public records in many jurisdictions throughout the United States. IA collects county, state, and federal public record filings and maintains other information data bases such as Sleuth, People Finder, and Business Finder, data bases that search for people, businesses, and other locator information.

• Prentice-Hall Legal and Financial Services, 15 Columbus Circle, NY, NY 10023. Provider of comprehensive public record information services worldwide. Information services include searching and retrieval of: UCC, corporate/limited partnership, court record, tax lien, real property, SEC, federal agency, and environmental information. Maintains on-line data base for asset or locator searching that contains more than 150 million public record filings from the county, state, and federal levels.

• Prentice-Hall On-Line (PHO). Using one search command, you can search the entire data base for all data types in all locations on a given individual or company. Summary screen provides all matches from which detail viewing can be selected.

• Prentice-Hall Legal & Financial Services. Provides due diligence, business background, and asset searching services using a combination of on-line searches and manual searches of liens and court records. The result is a comprehensive report on the assets, liens, and liabilities of a given individual or business entity.

• Prentice-Hall Information Link (PHIL). Available with Prentice Hall On-Line, this on-line service is a host for thousands of scientific, technical, and business data bases. PHIL provides on-line access to more than 800 professional publications.

• TRW—REDI-DATA, 1700 NW 66th Avenue, Ft. Lauderdale, FL 33313. A national real estate data base that collates the records of the county tax assessor to list the owners and tax payers of real property along with the address, legal description, and tax-assessed value of the subject's property. This data base allows the investigator to search real estate ownership statewide in many jurisdictions rather than county by county, as is available from most other sources.

WITH A COMPUTER AND THE RIGHT PERIPHERALS, VIRTUALLY NO INFORMATION IS BEYOND YOUR REACH.

EQUIPMENT NEEDED TO ACCESS PUBLIC RECORDS

The three greatest investigative tools of modern time are the telephone, computer, and fax machine. These tools give you instant access to the world of spoken and written communications, as well as bringing you the wonderful world of public information right to your door.

Computer

With today's modern price wars and glut of personal computers, any investigator can afford a world-class computer setup for under $2,000. Just pick up the ads in any Sunday newspaper or computer magazine and you will become barraged with choices from Apple, Compaq, and Dell to Radio Shack and Texas Instruments. The choice of computer is up to you, but I would recommend one that has quick and dependable service through a nearby repair and maintenance facility.

When buying a computer, you should consider both the price and the availability of service. Again, make sure that you have a repair facility nearby that can perform any needed maintenance or troubleshoot any problems that you have getting your system up and running. If you pick up your local newspaper or computer magazine, you'll see all the brands and prices, duking it out in their most recent price war. Here are a few brands that I recommend you look at, to help you in your choice.

—IBM PS/1 Model 2123
—Compaq Prolinea 3/25S 386SX/25MHz
—Dell 486P/33 486/33MHz
—Dell 333P 386/33MHz
—Packard Bell 486-DX 33 MHz
—Packard Bell 386-SX 20 MHz
—Leading Edge 80486 DX/50 MHz
—Leading Edge 80386 DH/33 MHz

Laptops

If you are into laptop computers, which are wonderful for frequent travelers who conduct business on the road, these are a few of several good choices:
—Compaq Contura 3/20 Model 84 386SL/20 MHz

—Leading Edge DNE 258-SX (386 processor)
—Toshiba T3300SL (386 processor)

By the time this book is published, the prices on the 486 series of computers will probably come down to where the 386s are today. If they do, my recommendation is to buy a 486 because it has the speed and power to run all of the wonderful new windows programs that make computer usage so idiotproof that even I can use them. If you have wondered why I picked IBM-compatible equipment over that of Apple, it's because there are many more IBM investigator users and much more software available for these systems. The Apple is certainly more user-friendly and has many graphics features not found in the IBM-compatible equipment, but most of the people in this business have gone to IBM-compatible equipment and are more familiar with its use (with new software available that lets Apples talk to IBMs, you can now use either kind of equipment and get the same results). If you are into computers and like all the toys, then there are a number of other goodies that you can add to your system to make it hum.

Modem

The one essential piece of additional equipment you want for your computer is a modem so that you can plug in to all of those wonderful informational data bases that make the computer more than a word processor. The term modem is an acronym for modulator/demodulator. This device translates letters, numbers, and other symbols into tones that can be carried on the telephone lines and translates the tones it receives back into letters, numbers, and symbols. Every communicating computer needs one so that you can talk to other computers. Dozens of companies now make modems, but the standard of the industry is the Hayes Smartmodem. Just be sure that any modem that you buy is "Hayes" compatible. My choice is a Hayes compatible 1,200- or 2,400-baud modem so that you can download your information in the wink of an eye.

Mouse

The mouse is almost nine years old and

still rolling along. Mice and the newer track balls facilitate using many programs. The mouse device makes the cursor responsive to hand movement rather than requiring you to enter F-key commands or number/letter combinations to perform tasks and operate programs. Many systems have built-in mouse controllers and plug-ins "on board" when purchased, or you can add a function board to your existing system. Window environments almost necessitate mouse operation for ease of use. Additionally, there are mouse pens, graphic tablets, joysticks, and something called the Unmouse that you use by sliding your finger around on a glass surface to manipulate the pointer. There are mouse devices for laptops also.

Internal Fax Board

There are pros and cons regarding the use of an internal fax board. They obviously take the place of stand-alone equipment and save having to print the document that you wish to create and transmit. Other positive features are no paper jams, several cover sheets stored for use, better image output on the receiving end, and the fact that you can haul your fax along when you take your computer on the road.

The downside to internal fax boards is that you have to have an optical character recognition system (scanner) in order to send copies of articles already in printed form. You have to leave your computer on in order to be able to receive a fax at any time (if you spend a lot of time on-line, your fax will be out of service while you are using your modem). You cannot edit incoming messages before printing without converting them to a text file using OCR software, and the background operating of the fax board may slow down or interfere with other computing tasks on a slow computer (below 12 MHz).

CD-ROM Disk Drive

One of the latest devices to arrive on the computer scene is the Compact Disk-Read Only Memory systems. CD-ROMs are just like the disks used to record music. At the moment, they have information stored on them, and you purchase them for "in house" use of vast information banks that do not need daily updating. Data bases that provide current information still must be accessed on-line. CD-ROMs function like encyclopedias or textbooks by furnishing a searchable environment on computer. Computers are now arriving on the market with CD-ROM drives installed, and the technology for all users to not only read but also to write to and file huge amounts of information on one disk is on the horizon.

Optical Character Reader

Until recently, OCRs, more commonly called scanners, were financially out of reach for the occasional user. Now, however, hand-held and full-page versions with attendant software are available and more favorably priced for the serious computer user.

OCRs allow you to "read" a printed page, photograph, picture, line art, or what have you into your computer system. You can save hours of data input and eliminate costly proofreading with such a device. Also in desktop publishing, it allows you to copy logos and designs that are specific to your material without having to go to a professional printer.

CREDIT REPORTS

Once a cottage industry of small mom-and-pop collection agencies, today's credit bureaus are dominated by three giant super bureaus that collect credit transactions and financial data on almost every person in America. The big three bureaus—TRW, TransUnion, and Equifax—have grown by acquiring the network of small local agencies and merging them into a national network under these three companies' ownership. The information that the credit bureaus provide comes from a variety of sources.

These sources include credit information reported from local and national businesses, government agencies that sell certain identification and financial information, and insurance companies and financial institutions that report information on insurance policies or parties applying for credit. All of the three big credit bureaus have information on millions of people. But each has an area of the country in which it has greater information coverage than its competitors. In the western states, TRW has the greatest coverage, with Trans Union having the most complete data in the central states and Equifax covering the eastern seaboard.

Often, it is wise to access all three of these data bases to make sure you acquire the most current, up-to-date information on a subject and the areas he has traveled through. In addition to its traditional credit reports, these bureaus provide a number of other services of tremendous value to the on-line investigator.

All of us are familiar with the term "credit report," but few people know exactly what one is and what it provides (see example at right). Many investigators are surprised to learn that the credit bureaus issue or sell a variety of reports that provide information outside credit status that does not fall under the guidelines of the Fair Credit Reporting Act (FCRA) and does not require a release of information or generate a credit inquiry notification, thereby informing the credit subject of your

Sample Report

```
I/CONSUMER/JOHN/E/2222/MAIN/JANE/444669999/77074/TY-P/RF-6 ❶

BUR-HOU ID-44443333 T-368 O-254 D-2/04/85 10.10.41 M-3-9999 KB-D ❷

   CREDIT BUREAU OF GR. HOUSTON ❸          SMITH DEPT INC ❹
   2505 FANNIN STREET
   HOUSTON, TX 77002
   ───────────────────
   CONSUMER, JOHN EDWARD ❺              ❻ SUBJECT SSN - 444-66-9999
   2222 MAIN ST                           SPOUSE NAME - JANE
   HOUSTON, TX 77074
   ───────────────────
ON FILE-12/78 BIRTH-10/54 DEPEND-3 CUR/ADR-SINCE-5/79,OWNS MAR-M ❼

EMPLOYER - COASTAL OIL CO ADDRESS - HOUSTON, TX ❽
   OCCUPATION - ACCOUNTANT HIRED - 10/80 VERIFIED - 4/82 INCOME - $ 2500

FORMER EMPLOYER - SELF ❾

FORMER ADDRESS - 1700 W MAIN APT 12, HOUSTON, TX ❿
⓫──⓭─────────── TYPE REPT-H OPEND HIGH/CR CURBAL PSTDUES-# MR 30 60 90❿
W    MEMBER NAME                      LST/P TRMS/PMT              MNTHS PSTDUE
 KB MEMB# ACCOUNT#
────────────────
1 ACS COLLECTIONS       OPN  4/32H 2/82   45     45    45-       MOP-9  $
  Y  89-88 #2345679-9                                            REMARKS-CLA

1 NAT STANDARD BK       INS  2/85A 12/82  12497  5210  1388-04   24 4 4 4$
  B  85-111 #32111133314397        1/85   347                    444322-11──

1 1ST NATIONAL BK       INS  2/85A 6/83   1575   340   00-00     10 0 0 0
  B  85-222 #233344400111AC        1/85   65                     0000000000──
                                                                REMARKS-DRP❷
O CASEY MENSWEAR        REV  6/84A 2/81   295    0     -         8 0 0 0
  CG 85-333 #938267                       45                     00000000──

2 SEARS                 INS  7/84A 1/80   45     0     00-00     14 2 0 0
  D  85-99999 #552444478                                         000-00001100

3 CORPUS CHRISTI,TX     REV  4/82M 4/77   300    200   00-       12 0 0 0
  D  90-99999 OOT/RPT-4/00/C2                                    000000000000

O FEDERAL SAVINGS       CHK  11/80M 3/80  LOW 4                  SATISFACTORY
  BB 10477 #98765

❷⑧TAX LIEN - 4/82 $6542 PARTY-STATE TX JOINT
   CASE-089-91-0423 CITY/STATE-HOUSTON, TX
   DISPOSITION-RELEASED

❷⑨ADDITIONAL INFORMATION
   9/84 LATE PAYMENTS ON 1ST NATIONAL BANK UNDER DISPUTE

❸⓪INQUIRIES --DATE-- WHS KOB MEMBER-NO  OTHER
              7/03/84  1   D   6504      JOSKES
              1/15/85  1   C   15138     NORTONS

❸⓵SUMMARY
   INQ OVR 90 DAY──1 INQ LST 90 DAY──1 PUB NEG RATED──1 TOTAL TRADES──6$
   TRDS POS RATED──4 TRDS NEG RATED──2 TRADE BANKS──2 TRADE DEPARTM──2
   TRADE OTHER──2 TRADE TYPE OPN──1 TRADE TYPE REV──2 TRADE TYPE INS──3
   TOTAL BANK SET──1 OLDEST TRADE──4/77 LATEST OPEN──6/83 OPN TR BAL──5795
   TOT TR PMT──412

❸⓶$END$
```

A SAMPLE CREDIT BUREAU REPORT GIVES INVESTIGATORS A LOOK INSIDE A SUBJECT'S FINANCIAL HISTORY.

request for information about his or her status. The types of reports provided by most credit reporting agencies in this area include:

• Social Security Trace. A search conducted to determine any name and address used by individuals who are recorded under a specific Social Security number. This search will give the various names and addresses reported to that Social Security number on credit applications and inquiries anywhere in their system (this search is the most cost-effective electronic means of locating individuals, with a "hit rate" of over 90 percent to a past or current

address and aliases used by a subject).

These searches also detect Social Security numbers that have been used for death claims and give the year it was filed. They also inform the searcher that a number has not been issued rather than just furnishing a "no record" report.

• Atlas Search. A computer-generated printout of the names, addresses, and telephone numbers of addresses surrounding the address given for your subject of investigation (see example on page 34). The data base also furnishes information from the National

```
                      SOCIAL SECURITY TRACE REPORT

                     MKT/SUB    INFILE    DATE      TIME
                      15 SC               10/16/92  10:53

RPT ON                            SSN        DOB
* SOCIAL SECURITY NUMBER TRACE *  460-13-0857
     NAME/SPOUSE                            SSN OWNER
     ADDRESS                                ADDR RPT DATE

1.   BRANTLEY, J T                          SUBJECT
     2951 MARINA BAY DR., LEAGUE CITY, TX.  77573   10/92
     803 W. MAIN ST., LEAGUE CITY TX.  77573
     16516 SEALARK, HOUSTON TX., 939  77062

2.   BRANTLEY, TODD                         SUBJECT
     2951 MARINE BAY DR., LEAGUE CITY TX.  77573   09/92
     803 W. MAIN, LEAGUE CITY TX.,939  77573       10/90
     16516 SEALARK, HOUSTON TX.,939  77062


3.   BRANTLEY, T J
     6609 SAXON, HOUSTON TX.,460   77018           08/89
     POB 2222, SPRING TX  77335                    01/88



     *** HAWK-ALERT:  CLEAR
     **END OF NETWORK TRACE**
```

EVERY PERSON IN THE UNITED STATES SHOULD HAVE A SOCIAL SECURITY NUMBER, ESPECIALLY WORKING PEOPLE.

Movers Index and U.S. Postal Service address forwarding information.

• Equifax Sleuth. To the computerized investigator, these searches are one of the most efficient and cost-effective means of locating individuals or addresses. A number of new data bases are now coming on-line that enhance this information by matching addresses to telephone numbers like an on-line criss-cross directory. Moving forward into the future, the credit bureaus are now acquiring additional data bases that contain additional information such as tax assessment records, postal change of addresses, and addresses reported to various governmental agencies that are sold by the government to these credit bureaus. Many of the credit bureaus are now denying membership to private investi-gators because they feel that the investigators will improperly use their services. To overcome this obstacle, you can explain to them that your use is strictly for legitimate purposes and that you will maintain on file (or fax them) a release in matters where you want a full credit report. For the other services that the credit bureaus provide, such as Social Security trace and Atlas search, no FCRA release is necessary. If worst comes to worst, sign up with the credit bureaus for Social Security trace and Atlas search, and then ask them to increase your services, once you have shown them that you are a legit-imate customer.

• Equifax Services, Inc., 1600 1 Peachtree Street, N.W., Atlanta, GA 30309.

• Transunion, 555 West Adams St., Chicago, IL 60661.

```
                    ATLAS SEARCH REPORT

                              DATE       TIME
                              10/16/92   10:54

**SUBJECT VERIFICATION WITH 5 NEIGHBORS**

G01I  BRANTLEY,J* 2951,MARINABAY,DR,LEAGUECITY,TX,77573**


ADDRESS
01.  LAVERELL HOWARD R      DU: SFDU  DOR:1990  (713) 334-3321
     2913 MARINER DR        LEAGUE CITY         TX  77573-9234

02.  MAXWELL RANDALL T       DU: SFDU  DOR:1987  (713) 334-2897
     2945 MARINER DR        LEAGUE CITY         TX  77573-9234

03.  INGRAM SAM             DU: SFDU  DOR:1989  (713) 334-0165
     2949 MARINER DR        LEAGUE CITY         TX  77573-9234

04.  PHILLIPS MARY          DU: SFDU  DOR:1979  (713) 334-2600
     2950 MARINER DR        LEAGUE CITY         TX  77573-9234

05.  JOHNSON BOBBY          DU: SFDU  DOR:1990  (713) 334-6501
     2952 MARINER DR        LEAGUE CITY         TX  77573-9234

**END OF ATLAS REPORT**
```

A SAMPLE ATLAS SEARCH REPORT GIVES OCCUPANTS OF SURROUNDING ADDRESSES.

• TRW Information Services, 901 N. International Parkway, Richardson, TX 75081.

COMMUNICATIONS AND MEDIA

The power of the written word has grown tremendously in the last 10 years through the advent of the computer. The mass of information reported in our newspapers, periodicals, journals, and magazines is now instantly available and can be accessed by name, subject, or circumstances by city, region, national, or global means. Through this access, the world-class con man can no longer outrun his past and stay ahead of his reputation by outrunning the "word of mouth" trail he leaves in his wake. In almost every jurisdiction, the local media has a tremendous resource of information that can enhance the investigator's capability dramatically.

On a recent investigation in New England, I was interviewed by Boston's *Banker & Tradesman* newspaper regarding the losses by financial institutions in New England. While touring the paper's offices, I met the director of computer data and determined that this newspaper owned five other New England publications and that, together, they had published all of the public record filings of court actions and real estate purchases from Connecticut to Maine from 1985 to the present. Having searched real estate transactions from township to township as they are stored in the public records, I was amazed and delighted to see that I could now access a five-state region through a central computer.

By searching in the name of my subject, his spouse's maiden name, and his mother's maiden name, we quickly identified more than 20 properties and cost-effectively completed a search within hours, not the weeks that we had anticipated in a manual search. As more of these regional data collectors merge their information into national resellers like Prentice Hall On-Line, Dialog, and Lexis/Nexis, the ease and cost of searching for information and assets will improve dramatically.

A brief list of a few of the many companies offering on-line communications and media materials is as follows:

• Information Access Company (IAC), 362 Lakeside Drive, Foster City, CA 94404. A provider of reference materials that gives periodical reference products, both on-line and through CD-ROM terminals, in thousands of North American libraries. IAC organizes the contents of major national and international publications into research data bases and draws from more than 4,000 national and international trade, business, health, and medical journals, as well as both local and global news wires.

•Magazine Index. Magazine Index is a data base of more than 370,000 major U.S. and Canadian magazines dating from 1979 to the present. (Access is through Dialog.)

• Mead Data Central, Inc., P.O. Box 993, Dayton, OH 45401. Mead Data Central is a data base that contains major newspaper, legal, government, and other publications. Its two most widely used data bases are Lexis (a large and widely used full-text legal data base containing cases from federal and state courts) and Nexis, a full-text data base consisting of general news, business, and financial information from more than 150 newspapers, with data from 1975 to present.

• Newsearch, Produced by Information Access Services. Newsearch provides access to the most current articles and wire stories from more than 1,800 newspapers, wire services, magazines, business publications, and computer and legal publications. It is the daily update for six data bases on Compuserve.

• Newsnet, 945 Haverford Road, Bryn Mawr, PA 19010. Newsnet maintains files through major newspapers, government publications, magazines, and newspapers that are broken down by sources and subjects. The topics include advertising, automotive, marketing, construction to law, public relations, real estate, social sciences, and many, many more.

• Data Times. Data Times is a major newspaper, magazine, periodical, and business information data base providing a vast amount of information from foreign publications as well as a majority of the 50 states. It also provides access to the complete Dow Jones News Retrieval Service.

• Standard and Poors, 25 Broadway, New York, NY 10004. Standard and Poors is a financially oriented data base providing information about 36,000 corporations and 340,000 "key executives" with more than 74,000 profile biographies. This data base also provides background and financial information on banks, savings and loans, and other financial institutions. Accessible through Dialog and Data Times.

• Vu-Text Information Services, Inc. Vu-Text Information Services is a data base containing information from over 500 publications that assist in locating articles on individuals and businesses throughout the United States. This company is currently merging with Dialog.

SCIENTIFIC AND TECHNICAL DATA BASES

The advance of scientific information and learning has been so rapid in recent years that only through the use of the computer could scientists keep up with the tremendous growth of knowledge available. This burst of knowledge has been electronically collated, processed, and stored and is now for sale for information resellers such as Dialog, Compuserve, and Meadata, companies that offer hundreds of technical information menus, easily accessible by subject, circumstances, or party being researched.

Data bases offered in these fields include agricultural, biographical, chemical, legal, medical, and technical areas, to mention just a few of the more than 500 fields of knowledge offered to subscribers. These scientific and technical data bases draw their information from professional and technical journals, professional papers, graduate theses, and government studies related to their specific fields. Through these data bases, the on-line investigator can quickly accumulate the technical knowledge necessary to support their suppositions.

• Compuserve Information Service, 5000 Arlington Center Blvd., Columbus, OH. This company is a worldwide information reseller of on-line information, communication, and reference data bases. Through Compuserve, clients can access more than 400 financial, communication, newspaper, and entertainment data bases. In addition, Compuserve maintains various member bulletin boards, fax, and E-Mail services.

• Dialog, P.O. Box 10010, Palo Alto, CA 94304. Offering access to more than 800 data bases, this company maintains more than 80 million records concerning directory, business, and financial data. Its records maintain information on many scientific and technical fields as well as provide access to major communication and directory service data bases.

• Information on Demand, Inc., 8000 W. Park Dr., McLean, VA 22102. A provider of on-line business news and specialty technical information for research facilities and government agencies. This company provides full text copy of any publicly available document, including technical reports, government documents, journal articles, patents, videocassettes, and conference proceedings. This company is an excellent technical source for biomedical information and patent and trademark records.

• Scorpio. A government data base accessed through the Congressional Research Service located in Washington, D.C. This service contains numerous data bases that provide abstracts of important government information, including the following:
—Library of Congress Computerized Catalog contains all books written in the English language since 1978.
—Bibliographic Citation File has selected citations to journal articles from 1976 to nowt that might be of interest to Congress.
—Congressional Status Files maintains information searched by subject or by bill number to determine the status of any bill.
—National Referral Center Master File is a

data base consisting of records of 14,500 trade organizations and professional societies and lobbies.

—Securities Information Center is operated by Itel Corporation under contract with the SEC to collate records regarding bad securities and other financial records relating to the banking and brokerage business.

—CAPCRIME Producer, CAP Index, Inc. This data base can be used to determine criminal justice statistics concerning how likely a crime is to occur at a given location. The company produces a model that gives current year and five-year projections of the likelihood of certain types of crime occurring in a particular geographic location. It has crime risk data for any U.S. location and can be used by security consultants and planners in analyzing the vulnerability of specific sites to crime.

FINANCIAL DATA BASES

• American Banker—Produced by American Banker-Bond Buyer, One State Street Plaza, New York, NY 10004. This is a daily production of the full text of all major news stories on banking and financial services. AB reports on the latest events affecting the industry throughout the United States and analyzes trends, technological innovations in banking and regulator activities in the industry. Available through Dialog, Mead Data, Newsnet, and Data Times.

• Business America On-Line. Produced by American Business Information, 5711 South 86th Circle, Omaha, NE 68127. A comprehensive business data base with information on more than 10 million companies, including company name, address, phone number, names of owners, employees, and sales volumes. The company provides business profiles, and market research information on a nationwide basis.

• Business Dateline. Produced by UMI/Data Courier. Collection of full-text stories on

major business issues drawn from more than 180 regional business periodicals throughout the United States and Canada. Collects data from local business journals throughout the United States and is an excellent source of information on small businesses and their financial activities.

• Disclosure, Inc., 5161 River Road, Bethesda, MD 20816. Provider of timely and accurate information relating to publicly traded companies and their officers and directors. Disclosure has an on-line index of every document filed with the SEC, covering more than 70 *Fortune* 500 public companies. This company also provides annual reports and monitoring services that follow the litigation, legislation, and stock activities of both national and some international public companies.

• Dun & Bradstreet Information Services, Three Sylvan Way, Parsippany, NJ 07054. This company provides on-line information regarding the financial history of corporations. My only caveat is that most of this information is self-reported except for corporate and UCC records. The company also provides microfiche containing listings that show business identities through assumed name corporate records nationwide.

• Investext. Produced by Thompson Financial Network. This company claims to be the world's largest international data base of company and industry research reports. The data base contains 320,000 reports on 21,000 companies and 53 industry categories. The company also draws from sources in Asia and Europe and produces industry, geographic, and topical reports on various business subjects. Accessible through Dialog, Compuserve, Dow Jones News, Mead, Lexis/Nexis, and Newsnet.

• Moody's Corporate Profiles. Produced by Moody's Investors Service. This data base contains concise descriptions and financial overviews of companies listed on the New York Stock Exchange and American Stock Exchange and many of the national over-the-counter exchanges. The information includes company descriptions, earnings, dividends, revenues, and other financial information. Accessible through Dialog.

PEOPLE AND MONEY
RELATED DATA BASES

A number of data bases have been created that are specifically designed to assist in professional investigators, collectors, and attorneys in locating people and other personal information. These data bases include the following:

• Agency Management Services (AMS), 3001 East Bypass, College Station, TX 77845. (800) 888-8553.

• American Data Research Inc., P.O. Box 17881, Salem, OR 97305. This company is a reporting bureau for the insurance industry that provides a full array of state motor vehicle information, both in the United States and in the Canadian provinces and in Puerto Rico.

• Disclosure On-Line. Produced by Disclosure, Inc. Disclosure collects information on more than 12,000 publicly held companies direct from annual and quarterly financial statements and reports as well as regulation statements filed with the SEC. These documents disclose assets, liabilities, stock prices, earnings, dividends, sales figures, and other financial business information. It is accessible through Dialog, Compuserve, Dow Jones News, Mead-Lexis, Routers, and Data-Star.

• Dow Jones News Retrieval Services. Produced by Dow Jones & Company. Articles and special features from financial magazines such as the *Wall Street Journal* and *Barrons*, along with information from the Dow Jones News Service (DJNS), also known as the "ticker." Searches can be conducted by stock symbol or name to follow business data on major corporations. Available through Dow Jones News, Dialog, and Data Times.

• Electronic White Pages. Produced by Regional Telephone Companies. An on-line electronic directory assistance service available for many parts of the United States listing over 120 million names, addresses, and telephone numbers. For locating people without other identifying information. This data base is hard to beat. Accessible through Directory Net, Inc.

• *Marquis Who's Who.* Biographies on more than 100,000 business executives listed in the various *Who's Who* directories produced by this company. An excellent source for personal background, educational, and other information concerning many prominent people in all fields of life. Accessible through Dialog and Compuserve.

• Metronet, 360 E. 22nd Street, Lumbard, IL 60148. This is an on-line system of locator information maintained by Metromail Corporation. Metronet provides on-line access to national consumer and change of address data bases for address verification, telephone look up, and neighbor look up.

• Phonefile. This is a Compuserve file (Go Phonefile) that is extrapolated from Metronet. It is a national data base of telephone directory information that can determine the current surname, location (city, state, or area code), or telephone number of any given name in its national data base. This data base is one of the most cost-effective locator resources and can be accessed through Compuserve at a fee of $.25 per minute. You must enter one request at a time. This is a cheap source of listed residential phone lists and for addresses that have nonpublished numbers. This data base allows you to set search results to scroll and down load for later review. Accessible through Compuserve.

• Standard and Poors' Register-Biographical. Produced by Standard and Poors. A biographical directory to more than 70,000 high-level American executives, listing personal data to include residence, birth place, year of birth, company affiliation, degrees, and other valuable information. Updated twice a year, this register gathers background information of executives in major U.S. industries. Available through Dialog, Mead, and Lexis/Nexis.

Computer Services Costs

All of the on-line information services have flexible fee schedules based on the volume of the user and the contract price negotiated with individual clients and government agencies. One rule of thumb that is common throughout the industry is that the costs are highest during peak usage times (8:00 A.M. to 6:00 P.M.) and substantially lower, often one-half, during off-peak usage hours.

One cardinal rule that I learned long ago was that you should always predetermine your information cost and know both what you are buying and what you are paying for. (I once ordered a Dun & Bradstreet Report on a major U.S. company and noted at the end of the report that I was billed $25 for the service. At the end of the report, I was asked if I wanted a "Family Tree" on this company. Not knowing the cost and presuming it would give me more information at a similar fee, I punched in a "Yes" and preceded to receive a 62-page report of business data relating to every entity owned by the company I was searching with a bill at the bottom of the page for $1,560. You can bet I was right on the phone calling the service bureau to explain that I really didn't need all that expensive information.)

Another thing to keep in mind is the closer you go to the actual producer of the information, the cheaper the cost. Every time you add another information reseller onto the food chain, a middle-man fee for the use of the services is added. It therefore behooves the computerized investigator to purchase as much information as possible from the direct seller and not from "super bureaus" that offer everyone else's services at an expanded fee. (A very good example is Dun & Bradstreet reports, which can cost as low as $25 when ordered directly from the company in volume. The same reports, ordered through Compuserve, cost more than three times as much but can be ordered individually rather than prepurchasing enough reports to last six months or a year.)

PI Networks— The Key to Education and Profit

I n every aspect of the investigative business, there are a number of professional associations that educate, train, and serve as a social outlet for those of us in the private investigation business. These associations provide a forum for letting others know of your existence and your expertise and will often be the best source of ideas when you run out of them. The more you put into these associations, the more you'll get out. Go to the meetings, send comments to their newsletters, and write up your most interesting case or new idea to share with your members. For every ounce of energy you put into the association, you'll get 10 back, one way or another.

FINANCIAL FRAUD INVESTIGATION

- International Association of Credit Card Investigators, 1620 Grant Ave., Novato, CA 94945.
- National Association of Certified Fraud Examiners, 716 West Ave., Austin, TX 78701.
- Institute of Internal Auditors, 249 Maitland Ave., Altamonte Springs, FL 32701.

INSURANCE INVESTIGATIONS

- International Association of Special Investigative Units, PO Box 8187, Madison, WI 53708.
- National Health Care Antifraud Association
- International Association of Insurance Fraud Agencies, Inc., 160 W. Broadway, #1928, New York, NY 10013

- International Association for Healthcare Security & Safety, Box 637, Lombard, IL 60148
- American Risk & Insurance Association, University of Georgia, 206 Brooks Hall, Athens, GA 30602

PHYSICAL SECURITY AND INVESTIGATION

- American Society of Industrial Security (ASIS), 1655 N. Fort Meyer Dr., Suite 1200, Arlington, VA 22209
- Security Industry Association, 1801 K St., N.W., Suite 1203L, Washington, DC 20006
- National Crime Prevention Institute, University of Louisville, School of Justice Administration, Shelby Campus, Louisville, KY 40292

PRIVATE INVESTIGATOR ASSOCIATIONS

- Council of International Investigators
- National Association of Legal Investigators (NALI), 2801 Fleur Drive, Des Moines, Iowa 50321
- National Association of Investigative Specialists (NAIS), P.O. Box 33244, Austin, TX 78764
- National Council of Investigative & Security Services (NCISS), Box 449, Severna Park, MD 21146
- World Association of Detectives (WAD), P.O. Box 1049, Severna Park, MD 21146
- Investigators On-Line Network (ION), 1920 West Lindner Ave., #201, Mesa, AZ 85202
- International Association of Arson Investigators

- International Association of Credit Card Investigators, 1620 Grant Ave., Novato, CA 94945
- Competitor Intell Association
- National Association of Public Record Researchers

PROCESS SERVICES

- National Association of Professional Process Servers

POTENTIAL CLIENT ASSOCIATIONS

- American Bankers Association, 1120 Connecticut Ave., N.W., Washington, DC 20036
- Association of Management Consulting Firms, 230 Park Ave., New York, NY 10169
- Bank Administration Institute, 60 E. Gould Ctr., Rolling Meadows, IL 60008
- Communications Security Association, 10060 Marshallpond Road, Burke, VA 22015
- International Council of Shopping Centers, 665 Fifth Ave., New York, NY 10022
- Property Management Association, 8811 Colesville Road, Suite G106, Silver Spring, MD 20910

In addition to investigator networks, every trade group has its own association that caters to its members and their suppliers. Once you develop a clear sense of what kind of business you want or develop an expertise that you want to bring to more clients, go to the library or bookstore and get one of the books listed in the Bibliography that tells you the associations and trade groups that cater to every industry.

8 Building the Investigative Library

ne of the smartest things an investigator can do, one that will save a lot of time and money, is to build an investigative library either at home or in the office. Wherever you do your work, if the information and tools are at your fingertips you can work a lot smarter than your competition. Putting together an investigative library isn't expensive; in fact, if you do it right, it might not cost you a dime. As you grow and bring more information into your library, your costs are going to go up, but the information will pay for itself many times over. (See the Bibliography for the basics every investigator's library should include.)

Contact your local lawyer and doctor or stop in at their professional societies, the local bar association, or medical society, while you are downtown one day and pick up a copy of their professional directories. These books give the full name, business and home address, unlisted residence telephone number, and photograph of every lawyer and doctor in your community. Once you're in business awhile, you'll know that the people you serve most often with witness subpoenas are doctors and lawyers, and they rarely accept processes at their offices. With a copy of their professional directories, you know right where they live and even have a picture to identify them when they tell you that they're not the ones.

TELEPHONE BOOKS

As you travel about in your business, collect every telephone book from every town that you travel through. These phone books give you business and personal names, addresses, and a list of other people in similar businesses that you can contact for information about the people you are investigating.

If you travel outside the United States to any of those places that the Beach Boys sing about in "Kokomo,"(Bermuda, Bahamas, Jamaica, Cayman Islands), be sure and bring back the phone books from these areas, as they list all of the offshore banks and lawyers that act as trustees for people doing business in those countries.

So you don't travel overseas or out of the country? Call up your telephone service representative and order copies of the phone books in the areas where you work or want to find business. It's cheaper than traveling and provides you with the information on everybody in that jurisdiction (you can now get both white-page and yellow-page information nationwide on a CD-ROM disk). This information is great for locating people nationwide and will help you find other investigators in areas that don't have any of your local association members. Another telephone resource is the AT&T 800 directory and the phone fax directory, which can be ordered from AT&T.

NEWSPAPER CLIPPINGS

The first private investigator I ever saw on TV had to be Paladin, the San Francisco gunslinger. Mr. Paladin read his newspaper religiously and tore out articles about people who needed his services and sent them his card. You too should read the newspapers and tear out the articles that offer not only potential marketing leads, but those that offer some information of value to you and your clients. In last week's *Wall Street Journal*, I read and tore out an article about an attorney being charged criminally for *not* advising his client not to wiretap his spouse, which is against the law. Both the husband and the attorney were charged with violating the federal wiretap statutes. I sent this article to all of the divorce or domestic relations attorneys I deal with, along with a brief cover letter so they should be aware of this important case. This gentle reminder of my skills and concern for their welfare brought in three new cases!

My office now collects all kinds of newspaper articles and saves them in manilla file folders under diverse headings ranging from applicant screening, banking, and child abuse to voice print technology. Whenever a client calls for information on voice print technology, I know right where the article is that tells about the technology developed by Dr. Kersta and can either fax it to his office or take the information to the attorney while he is meeting with his client, a person who may need my services as well.

REFERENCE BOOKS

As an avid reader, and now writer, I try to collect everything in print that has any relationship to my business. Ideas for reference books that you may want to follow run something like this:

• *Black's Law Dictionary*, 5th Edition 1979, by Henry C. Black, (West Publishing Co., St. Paul, MN). An excellent reference to the language of the law and the translation of the legal terms that appear in many of our legal documents.

• *Black's Medical Dictionary*, edited by C.H. Havard (Barnes & Noble Books, Sabage, MD). This dictionary defines and explains a wide range of terms and concepts used in medicine and related subjects, such as anatomy, physiology, pathology, etc.

• *Investigator's Guide to Sources of Information*, U.S. General Accounting Office (Office of Special Investigations), U.S. Government, GAO/OSI 92-1. This guide was printed for government investigators to help them locate all of the sources of information available from public records, government agencies, and other sources. As a freebie, or at minimal cost from your government printing office, this book is a steal and should be in every library.

• *Physician's Desk Reference* (PDR), 46th Edition, 1992 (Medical Economics Data, Oradell, NJ). The PDR is the standard reference book for anyone involved in the medical profession. In this book, you can look up drugs by product name, manufacturer, category, chemical, or generic name and examine a full color actual-size photographic index of the most commonly prescribed drugs. (When a client brings you the drugs used by their children, you can appear to be a rocket scientist by quickly identifying those strange pills.)

• *Gale's Encyclopedia of Associations*. This book lists each chartered public and private association in the United States and some in foreign countries. It provides valuable information about an association's location, officers, and how to access their membership.

• *Directories in Print 1991*. This publication describes in indexes more than 14,000 directories of all kinds, including business, professional, industrial, and scientific rosters, as well as other lists and guides.

• *Traffic Accident Investigation Manual*, 9th Edition, 1986, Written by J.S. Baker and Lynn B. Fricke (Northwestern University Traffic Institute, Evanston, IL). This is considered the "bible" of accident investigation and is one of the easiest manuals to understand when it comes to accident investigation cases. This book deals with accident reconstruction, cause analysis, and other subjects that helps the investigator to interpret accident data.

• *Find It Fast*, 2nd Edition, by Robert I. Berkman (Harper & Row, New York, NY, 1990). To go through the information search process, from defining your problem to getting an expert to review the accuracy of your findings, this is the book. The newest edition offers information on electronic information services, research problems, and hundreds of new sources to find information about the esoteric case that some crazy attorney just brought you.

• *The MVR Book* (BRB Publications, Inc., Denver, CO). This book details and summarizes the descriptions, access, automation, and regulations of state driver and vehicle records and how to access this information nationwide.

ASSOCIATION DIRECTORIES

You should certainly consider association directories if you do business in those areas. A few examples are the state directories of realtors, nurses, insurance agents, law enforcement personnel, and notary publics. Each of these is available in some form through your state and is a true gold mine when you have to locate people in those fields. (Our firm once had to locate 300 former employees of a nursing home whose management was charged with murder for neglecting its patients. With RN and LVN directories in hand, we were able to locate virtually all of the 300 former employees and interview them within 60 days. Without this resource, we might not have gotten the case because the client's budget could not have afforded the old gumshoe methods of tracking down each nurse individually.

MICROFICHE/MICROFILM/CD ROM DISC

Some records haven't been computerized yet but are available on microfiche or microfilm. A prime example of this in many jurisdictions is the voter registration index, which lists the millions of voters in your county by name, address, date of birth, and Social Security number. This microfiche database is the single best source for locating people in your jurisdiction and is especially valuable when an attorney sends you 20 witness subpoenas at five o'clock on Friday afternoon that have to be served by Monday morning—and, of course, all the addresses are three years old and the courthouse is closed. By having these microfiche in house, you can make a minor miracle happen and collect a sizable fee that you otherwise might have missed.

For every area of investigation and security, there are literally hundreds of books written that add to the body of knowledge of our industry. I can't begin to go into all of the books here, but I have listed many of them in my bibliography at the back of this book. All I can say is that I try to collect every book I can because I learn something from every one of them. If I get one good idea out of an article, book, or seminar, then I feel that it is worth the price I paid many times over.

Locating People

Possibly the easiest, cheapest, and most profitable work a private investigator can do is to locate missing people, or skip-trace as it is known in the business. The business of locating missing witnesses, heirs, defendants, or family members is one of the most sought-after skills of a private investigator and is the one that, used properly, can return the greatest reward for efforts produced.

Unlike with surveillance or undercover operations, which require an hour's work for an hour's billing, many private investigators find they can charge a flat fee for locating people and reap a greater reward for their time, often without having to leave their home or office. You see, with the advent of the computer and the proliferation of on-line data bases, skip-tracing has truly come into its own as a marketable service that literally everyone needs sometime in their lives. Who are the people that most often use this service? Let me name a few.

• Banks. The collection or "workout" department of every financial institution in the country has a growing number of files for which it has been unable to find the debtor and either contact him or her by phone for collection purposes or serve them with court papers for nonpayment of debt. This kind of client has very high-volume needs and is often willing to give you dozens or even hundreds of cases if you can do the service cost effectively. (Early on in my career, I picked up 300 such files at an agreed price of $200 each, thus producing $60,000 over a six-month period.)

• Attorneys. This is the largest potential market for locator services because attorneys file the lawsuits that require personal service on unlocated debtors. They will also hand you 20 papers with bad address-

```
┌─────────────────────────────────────────────────────────────────┐
│              INTERTECT, INC.  -  LOCATE FORM                      │
│  CASE # _____ AGENT _____ DATE _____    │
│  SUBJECT _____ │
│  ADDRESS _____ CITY _____ ST/ZIP _____     │
│  DOB _____ SS# _____ SPOUSE _____     │
├─────────────────────────────────────────────────────────────────┤
│  TELEPHONE BOOK                                                   │
│  CRISS CROSS DIR.                                                 │
│  VOTER REG.                                                       │
│  ASSUMED/CORP NAMES                                               │
│  ELECTRIC/UTILITY                                                 │
│  WATER/GAS UTILITY                                                │
│  DRIVERS LICENSE                                                  │
│  CREDIT /SS TRACE                                                 │
│  EMPLOYMENT/LICENSING BOARDS                                      │
│  STATE EMPLOYMENT COMMISSION                                      │
│  NOTARY REGISTRATION                                              │
│  POST OFFICE (FOIA REQUEST)                                       │
│  MARRIAGE/DIVORCE  RECORDS                                        │
│  CIVIL SUITS & ATTY                                               │
│  CRIMINAL RECORDS & BONDSMAN                                      │
│  UCC'S & BANK                                                     │
│  REAL PROPERTY                                                    │
│  NEWSPAPER INDEX                                                  │
├─────────────────────────────────────────────────────────────────┤
│     *** ATTACH COPIES OR WRITTEN INFORMATION TO THIS REPORT ***   │
│  EX SPOUSE _____ FORMER EMPLOYER _____       │
│  FAMILY MEMBERS _____ FORMER CO-WORKER _____       │
│  FAMILY MEMBER _____ FORMER BANKS _____       │
│  NEIGHBORS _____       │
└─────────────────────────────────────────────────────────────────┘
```

A COPY OF INTERTECT'S LOCATE FORM.

es at 5:00 on Friday afternoon and expect you to locate and serve all of the parties by 9:00 Monday morning (for this you charge extra).

• Insurance Companies. You try to read the witnesses' names or find their addresses on an accident report! The insurance company sure can't and will therefore welcome your assistance in locating those people who saw the accident a different way or were present when the moving van was loading Fred's most prize possessions on a truck the night before the fire burned down his home.

• Private Individuals. Everyone has a long-lost friend, lover, or enemy whom they dream of finding someday. You could make their dreams come true by placing an ad in their high-school-reunion announcements or one of the many suburban or underground newspapers that cater to the personal interests of the lovelorn. Whatever the reason, every single person you talk to has somebody that he or she wants to find, and most have no idea how inexpensive it can be to find him or her.

A smart investigator wishing to capitalize on this business will set a flat fee for locates (based on costs, overhead, and prior success rates) and find a magic number like $250 as a fee to locate the person's heart's desire. To make this service successful, you have to be both good at your work and find a clientele base with a volume of business so that the eight easy locates you find in one hour compensate for the two motengators (an old Texas term that means "big gators") that you stay up three nights searching for.

To become a skip-tracing whiz, you need only three tools: a telephone, computer (complete with on-line data bases), and fax machine. These tools are the same basic building blocks needed in every other phase of prudent private investigation and are the building blocks of any good investigator's bag of tricks.

The next thing needed is an action plan that makes you and your staff follow a prescribed methodology that has proven to be successful for thousands of skip-tracers all over the country. To make it easy for you, I've condensed the most logical and cost-effective steps in conducting skip-tracing onto one simple form that, if followed, will work for you every time. If you follow the steps on this form in the order given or as close to it as you can come, then you are on your way.

CHAPTER 10

Manhunting— Reach Out and Touch Someone

Nowhere in the investigative industry is the impact of technology as dramatic as in the field of finding people who don't want to be found. Through computers and the collation of data on every credit and security transaction we conduct, it's almost impossible for people to hide their electronic signatures from those who would sniff them out and track them down. The key to locating people, whether they have disappeared by accident or on purpose, is to make a good checklist that starts with the easiest and most cost-effective searches and progresses to harder to obtain and more expensive information as the search goes on.

By knowing people's habits and having their initial identifying information, such as date of birth, Social Security number, and a former address, it is a relatively simple matter for you to find out either where the person being investigated is today or where he or she was at some point in time and then track him or her through friends, family, or business. In the words of the learned philosopher John Donne, "No man is an island, entire unto itself . . ." Each of us has our own network of personal, social, and business relationships that we rarely give up, no matter what we do or where we go. A good example of these relationships is described below.

Jack Snow was a witness to an arson for profit case and could testify to the fact that he was paid to bulldoze over a building slab with his tractor to help make the burned out building a total loss. Two other investigators tried to track Jack down, but neither of them searched the UCC records in his home county, which would have quickly shown that Jack had taken out a loan with Beneficial Finance Company and paid it off over a period of months before he left town. The shrewd investigator, who found the trail to the loan company by finding the

VOTER REGISTRATION APPLICATION *(SOLICITUD PARA REGISTRO DE VOTANTE)*

PLEASE COMPLETE ALL OF THE INFORMATION BELOW. PRINT IN INK OR TYPE. *(POR FAVOR COMPLETE LA SIGUIENTE INFORMACION ESCRIBA EN LETRA DE MOLDE CON TINTA O ESCRIBA A MAQUINA)*

Last Name *(Apellido)*	First Name (NOT HUSBAND'S) *(Nombre de Pila) (NO DEL ESPOSO)*	Middle Name (If any) *(Segundo Nombre) (si tiene)*	Maiden Name *(Apellido de Soltera)*
SMITH	ROBERT	ALLEN	

Sex *(Sexo)*	Date of Birth *(Fecha de Nacimiento)*	Place of Birth *(Lugar de Nacimiento)*		County and Address of Former Residence *(Condado y direccion de su residencia previa)*
		city or county *(ciudad o condado)*	state or foreign country *(estado o pais extranjero)*	
M	01/23/45 month, day, year *(el mes, el dia, el año)*	HOUSTON	TEXAS	HARRIS COUNTY

Permanent Residence Address: Street Address and Apartment Number, City, State, and ZIP. If none, describe location of residence. (Do not include P.O. Box or Rural Rt.) *(Dirección de Residencia Permanente: Calle y Número de Departamento, Ciudad, Estado, y Zona Postal; si no tiene, describa la localidad de su residencia. No incluya su caja postal o ruta rural.)*

1001 2ND ST., HOUSTON, TEXAS 77007

Social Security Number *(Numero de Seguro Social)*
123-45-6789

Mailing Address, City, State and ZIP: If mail cannot be delivered to your permanent residence address. *(Dirección Postal, Ciudad, Estado y Zona Postal) (si es imposible entregar correspondencia a su dirección permanente)*

314 Home Way, Houston, TX 77056

Telephone Number (Optional) *(Numero de Telefono) (No obligatorio)*   (713) 977-5671

Precinct Number (If known) *(Numero de precinto) (si lo sabe)*

The applicant is a citizen of the United States and a resident of this county. Applicant has not been finally convicted of a felony or, if a felon, is eligible for registration under Section 13.001(a)(4) of the Texas Election Code. I understand that the giving of false information to procure the registration of a voter is a misdemeanor. *(El suplicante es ciudadano de los Estados Unidos y es residente de este condado. El suplicante no ha sido probado culpable finalmente de un crimen, o, si es criminal, está elegible para registrarse para votar bajo las condiciones de la Sección 13.001(a)(4) del Código de Elecciones de Texas. Yo entiendo que es un delito menor dar información falsa con motivo de conseguir el registro de un votante.)*

X   *Robert A. Smith*

Signature of Applicant or Agent or Printed Name of Applicant if Signed by Witness *(Firma del Suplicante o Agente, o Nombre del Suplicante En Letra de Molde Si Fue Firmado Por Un Testigo)*

Court of Naturalization, If Applicable *(Corte de Naturalizacion, Si Aplicable)*

FOR AGENT *(PARA AGENTE)*: Application may be made by agent, who must be a qualified voter of this county or have submitted a registration application and must otherwise be eligible to vote and must be the applicant's husband, wife, father, mother, son or daughter *(La solicitud podrá estar dirigida por un agente que deberá ser un votante capacitado de este condado o que habrá presentado una solicitud para registrarse para votar, y de otro modo deberá de estar elegible para votar. El agente deberá ser el esposo, esposa, padre, madre, hijo o hija del suplicante.)*

Relationship *(Parentesco)* _____

FOR WITNESS *(PARA TESTIGO)*
Signature *(Firma)* ___ Check here if applicant is unable to make mark *(Marque aqui si el suplicante no puede hacer su marca)*   Printed name *(Nombre En Letra de Molde)*   Address *(Direccion)*

* The disclosure of social security number is voluntary. It is solicited by authority of Sec. 13.122 and will be used only to maintain the accuracy of the registration records *(No es obligatorio dar su numero de seguro social. Se solicita bajo la autoridad de la Sec. 13.122 y se usara solamente para mantener la exactitud de los archivos.)*

VOTER REGISTRATION RECORDS ARE THE LARGEST DATA BASES IN EACH STATE AND OFTEN ARE THE FIRST ONES COMPUTERIZED AND UPDATED.

record of the loan that Jack made, was able to speak to the manager of Beneficial Finance Company about Jack's loan. You see, it seems that Jack paid off the loan in Houston but requested that his loan file be transferred to Tabb, Virginia, so that Jack would have a source to borrow money already established at his new home. With the lead of Tabb, Virginia, it was easy to check phone and utility records in his new city and verify Jack's address with the Beneficial loan office, which was only too happy to verify Jack's credit and status with another company that was considering doing business with him.

FAMILY MEMBERS

One of the best pretexts that works almost every time on family members is the high-school-reunion pretext. It seems today that everybody is having a high school reunion, be it their fifth, tenth, twentieth, twenty-fifth, or thirtieth reunion. Everybody is trying to find their old friends from high school, college, or military service unit so that they can get together to see if Mary still fits into that high school letter sweater or if your old arch rival has really gone bald and lost his teeth.

VOTER REGISTRATION FILES

The next step in your manhunting exercise is to search the largest, most diverse data base in any county or state, filings of millions of persons in any major metropolitan area, a data base that lists family members, dates of birth, Social Security numbers, and most current addresses: the voter registration files.

In many counties, voter registration records are the first ones computerized so that local politicians can determine who is going to win the vote. They don't know it, but they are also providing a data base that indicates their voters' current and past addresses, dates of birth,

Social Security numbers, and signature samples—information that is vital to investigators.

To access these records, all you have to do is go to the county courthouse and ask for the office of the voter registration clerk. This office provides an alphabetical listing of all registered voters in that jurisdiction and also has microfiche or microfilm copies of the actual voter registration card, which often has signature samples and telephone numbers, right there before your very eyes, on the voters' registration forms. In response to the growing informational needs of skip-tracers, investigators, and creditors, many credit bureaus have tailored products once used to grant credit or market new customers to tracking people down.

Several credit companies now offer "header information" from credit bureau reports that lists the name, Social Security number, last employment, and credit inquiries on the individuals of your choice. These searches do not fall under the Fair Credit and Reporting Act because they don't provide credit information; they only identify information that assists the investigator and his client in locating where the public records or credit bureau last had contact with the subject of the search. One of the very best search products offered by any of the major credit bureaus is the "Social Security Trace Option," which searches the files of credit bureaus to determine the name and last credit granting or employment address of the Social Security number given.

By running this search at a nominal cost in most jurisdictions, an investigator can determine not only the most recent address of the person being sought, but also if the name matches the Social Security number given and if an insurance death claim was filed under that Social Security number. Through this type of search, we have found many people living under false names and Social Security numbers who otherwise would have gone undetected in our investigation.

AUTOMOBILE AND DRIVER'S LICENSE

Once you have a date of birth or Social Security number, it's a very easy matter to search driver's license records in almost all 50 states to determine if your subject is a registered driver. Most states access driver's license information by name and date of birth, but other states use the individual's Social Security number as their driver's license number, thus making it easier to find their subjects. When searching for the current last name of a woman or trying to chase her through several marriages, please note that the two things that don't change in a woman's life are her Social Security number and driver's license number (if kept within the same state). By searching under these identifiers, you can often get other married names and track back to a maiden name, which is usually issued in the same state as her Social Security number.

EMPLOYMENT COMMISSION AND LICENSING BOARDS

Another offshoot of the wonderful technology of the computer is the collation of worker's compensation claims filed by professional plaintiffs and injury-prone individuals all over the country. One company storing such data, the Industrial Foundation of America, collects compensation injury claims from employers and stores this information on a data base to sell to other members who sign up for its services in checking on insurance claims of injury-prone individuals.

While many businesses use this data base as a means to screen new applicants, I have found that it's also an excellent tool in locating people in high-risk or injury-heavy occupations, as well as those people who use their employers' workers compensation plan as a retirement benefit. In this same vein, people who work within a profession that requires licensing, registration, or bonding are often very easy to find if you know just where to look. Doctors, lawyers, police officers, engineers, plumbers, notary publics, and, yes, even private investigators and law enforcement officers are registered with their professional associations by name, business (and, frequently, home) address, telephone number, and fax number.

Many of these associations put out a directory that includes an identifying photograph

LICENSING BOARDS EXIST IN EVERY STATE FOR A NUMBER OF PROFESSIONS, RANGING FROM DOCTORS AND LAWYERS TO HAIR DRESSERS AND ANTIQUE DEALERS. THESE ARE A WONDERFUL SOURCE OF INFO FOR INVESTIGATORS.

so that when you go up to that doctor's door you found through the Medical Association Directory, you can be sure you are serving the right person with the malpractice lawsuit he's been evading at his office for more than six months. Something that I get calls for every month and could easily become an important part of your business is locating people who were witnesses to file documents, usually deeds, wills, or financial statements filed with a bank. (Did you know that it's now a criminal offense to file a fraudulent financial statement with an FDIC-insured institution?)

Who are the people who usually witness these documents? Of course, they're notary publics, the ones who stamp the documents with their seals and sign their names somewhere down around the bottom of the papers. If you want to find a specific notary or determine if the document is a legitimate one, just hunt up the notary both to verify his or her signature and also to look in the notary log to see if and when he or she actually witnessed and signed the document in question. How do you find him or her? I thought you'd never ask.

Every notary is required by various state laws to have a fidelity bond, usually from $2,000 to $10,000, on file with the state in which they are a notary. Both the state notary board and the bonding agency issuing the bond will have a recent or up-to-date address of your notary and will be responsive to your requests to locate them by simply picking up that wonderful investigative tool, the telephone, and calling them at their offices in the state capital.

SOCIAL ASSOCIATIONS

What if your subject is not employed, moves from job to job every time he gets wound up, gets fired, or is a general lowlife who isn't worth the attention of any professional association licensing board or regulatory agency? Well, the way to get him is through his sport or recreation. All of us, in some way or another, find a way to get away from it all, blow off steam, or generally just have a good time by going fishing, hunting, skiing, gambling, or something that we consider fun. We all find a way to get away, either in our minds or our bodies, from the daily grind of our lives and our jobs and usually take these sports much more seriously than our jobs.

Tony Arnetti, while working on a heavy

crane, sustained an injury by falling 12 feet into a pit he dug. After 10 days in the hospital and a month of rehabilitation, company doctors declared him fit for work. Instead of showing up at the job, Tony filed suit and disappeared. Claiming crippling injuries, Tony made a multi-million-dollar claim. His new address was listed as his brother in Milwaukee, but somehow his employer could never make personal contact with Tony at the address either in person or by phone. Surveillance of the given address disclosed no Tony or signs that he was around. Going back to the company personnel file, investigators read that Tony was a bowler and had in fact bowled on two company bowling leagues.

This lead generated a call to the American Bowling Congress (ABC) in Paramus, New Jersey, the official guardian of league bowling averages everywhere. The ABC records showed that not only was Tony still a league bowler, but that he bowled in a league in Minneapolis some hundred miles from Milwaukee. The records also showed the name of Tony's bowling partners and the fact that he hadn't missed a week of league since he filed his lawsuit.

Tony was a great witness in court, he told the jury of his months and years of pain and suffering, his inability to walk or move normally, and his diminished capacity as a husband and father due to his terrible fall. It's a shame that the next two witnesses were the custodian of records of ABC and the investigator who made the videos of Tony bowling a 600 series at the league finals. If not for them, Tony could have retired in grand style instead of facing a fraud claim.

As you are beginning to see, you cannot run, you cannot hide. As long as your subject maintains the same identity, he or she can be traced city by city, state by state, and often throughout the world. With today's technology and a good checklist (such as the one below), you can cut down your time in locating people from days to hours and minutes.

SOURCES OF INFORMATION CHECKLIST FOR FINANCIAL FRAUD

1. Telephone Records
   A) Business
   B) Personal
   C) Mobile Phone
   D) Pager

2. Telex Records

3. Overnight Packages (Federal Express, UPS, etc.)

4. Hotel Statements (Telephone Calls)

5. Expense Account Statements (Internal)

6. Credit Card Statements (External)

7. Credit Reports (Inquiries)

8. On-Line Newspaper Data Bases

9. Magazine Subscription Lists

10. TECS/EPIC (Foreign Travel Documentation)

11. CTR Report (Large Cash Transactions)

12. Air Travel—Airline Reporting Corp. (ARC)

Searching for Hidden Information and Assets

n today's business environment, with the escalating number of failed financial institutions and the continuing spiral of litigation, many investigators find that their time is devoted to determining the financial worth of individuals and businesses. Today's investigators search a wide variety of public record sources to include courthouse records, financial documents, and on-line computer data bases to help them determine if a party has sufficient assets to justify litigation or if any assets are being hidden from the creditors or lenders of a borrower.

Fortunately for the investigator, almost every transaction conducted today is a matter of public record. Everything we do is recorded, from our daily credit card transactions to our voter registration and marriage records to our business registrations, lawsuit history, and real estate purchases and sales. Each of the activities that we conduct, both in our private and public lives, are filed and recorded both to protect and guarantee our rights and to provide a public record to protect the interests of creditors, lenders, and others doing business with us in our daily activities.

The collection of the various types of data available in the public domain has become an art in itself. A growing number of private investigators and information brokers specialize in the development of information to assist their clients in making new business decisions, in locating assets in debt matters, and determining the business background and financial ability of people that their clients are considering as future business associates. The very same information and procedures are used to do an asset search for a lender and to locate assets in a debt. It is just a matter of viewpoint or focus in conducting the various types of investigations or examinations that lead us to different conclusions or answers. The key to beginning an investigation of this type is to know and understand the various types of public records available in your area of searching and how they can be used.

In every area of this country, and almost every other country in the world, there are a number of public records available that assist the investigator in developing clues. In the United States, the most readily available and informative place to start is the records of the county in which a person lives or does business. The county record offices (or county clerk's office) are the single greatest collector of public records of their constituents and are the jurisdiction for the filing of the majority of our personal and business activities.

Beginning an investigation of any type, the first information necessary to undertake an examination is to identify the party being investigated. Assuming that the party is an individual, or that he is investigating individuals who are affiliated with a business or company, then the investigator's first step is to view the public record resources that provide the information to properly identify the party he is examining. The sources that provide this identification are telephone records, voter registration, and marriage records.

TELEPHONE SOURCES

Among the greatest investigative tools available to virtually everyone are the various telephone directories and criss-cross directories that list the names, addresses, and telephone numbers of people having telephone listings in their local white or yellow pages directories. Every good investigator collects telephone directories so that he can search for the new and old addresses of parties he is investigating and find family members or others with the same last names to contact and use as a resource.

MARRIAGE LICENSE RECORDS PROVIDE A WEALTH OF INFORMATION: SPOUSE, ADDRESS AT TIME OF APPLICATION, PROOF OF CITIZENSHIP, AND THE FEMALE'S MAIDEN NAME.

VOTER REGISTRATION RECORDS

Voter registration records are collected from the registration of people voting in a county's jurisdiction and include such information as the full legal names, addresses, dates of birth, and Social Security numbers of persons voting in a given county. These records may also reveal a telephone number, unlisted with the telephone company but written on the voter registration application, and they provide signature samples of the voters that can be compared against other documents to verify the identity of the subject of investigation.

The voter registration records also collate all registrants alphabetically and provide the investigator with a list of people with the same last name as his or her subject's, thereby assisting in locating other parties who may have knowledge of the one being investigated. Often, we find that the individual being investigated is not registered as a voter, but the spouse or children are registered as voters at the very same address.

While examining voter registration records, the investigator should look for known spouses' or children's names or look for other parties at the same address known to once have been an address of the subject. By having this information, the investigator can then conduct a search for the spouse as well as the subject and have twice the chance of being successful.

MARRIAGE RECORDS

Marriage records document the union of two people in holy matrimony and document their identity by requiring dates of birth, Social Security numbers, and proof of identity. The proof of identity of U.S. citizens is frequently their driver's licenses, while persons of foreign extraction will usually use their passports, which is then listed on the record as documentation of their legal identities.

Marriage records also record both the maiden and married names of female spousal members. This provides the investigator with another name, one that is frequently used to hide business activities. (Many of the people found defrauding their employers and others trying to hide assets from creditors use their spouses' maiden names as vehicles to register businesses or sell property to.) By knowing the maiden name, a good investigator can make this connection and solve an otherwise difficult case. Once the individuals in an investigation are identified, the asset-searching investigator then can determine the business entities recorded in their names.

CORPORATIONS

In most jurisdictions, there are two types of business entity filings: corporate and assumed name, or Doing Business As (DBA) records.

The formation of corporations are recorded by the secretary of state in each state and sometimes in each county as well. The secretary of state requires the persons involved in forming a corporation to provide a list of the registered agent, incorporators, and the officers and directors of a corporation doing business in their states. In many states, these parties are also required to file financial statements that detail the amount of business conducted by the business entity.

To obtain this information, the investigator can examine the records of the secretary of state at the state capital or obtain copies of the information recorded by requesting it from the secretary of state. In many states, this information is now computerized and available through on-line information brokers that offer this information to their subscribers.

Assumed Name or DBA Records

These are the listings of individuals or companies registering a business name in a county, both to protect their right to use a name from others wishing to use the same name in that county, and to provide a record for lenders to verify the ownership of that business name in that county. Before any business can open an account at a bank, it must provide a copy of the corporate charter or assumed name certificate to prove that it has the right to use that name. In many jurisdictions, these records are listed alphabetically so that the researcher can determine each and every business name registered in an individual's name and determine each of the entities under which he or she is doing business in that jurisdiction. Once the investigator has determined the identifying information of the individuals and the business names used by them, the next step is often to determine their litigation histories.

I'LL SEE YOU IN COURT

The examination of legal actions or law-

DBA RECORDS ARE OFTEN LISTED ALPHABETICALLY IN THE OWNERS' NAMES, MAKING THE INVESTIGATOR'S JOB MUCH EASIER.

great deal of information not found through any other means.

Lawsuits are recorded in several different levels or jurisdictions to include county, state, and federal courts. The prudent investigator must search the courts at each level to determine the full extent of litigation filed on behalf of or against the person he is investigating. The following is a brief list of examples that will help the investigator understand the value of these records.

1. *Divorce lawsuits* often record the list of assets and liabilities of both the husband and wife, the division of property at the time of divorce, and a listing of properties or assets in jurisdictions outside that county. These records also provide the name of former spouses, witnesses such as friends, relatives, accountants, or business partners, and the record of bank accounts, insurance policies, and properties acquired both prior to and during the time of the marriage. These records may also list assets obtained through inheritance and will point the investigator to other areas of the country to search for clues.

2. *Business litigation lawsuits* record the disagreements between partners, as well as disputes between a company and its creditors, vendors, or employees, and will provide the investigator with a list of people who have knowledge of the business activities of the person under investigation. A search of these lawsuits may provide a list of previously used business names, names of associated business entities, and records of the financial payments

suits brought about by individuals or companies making claims against your subject of investigation often provide a detailed, documented record of the borrowing history, financial relationships, and assets of the person being investigated. By examining the records of other parties involved in litigation with your subject, you can quickly determine a

```
=N                    CIVIL NAME INQUIRY   **DCOY**       PAGE - 01
LAST NAME: KIRK_____  FIRST NAME: PAUL___
MIDDLE NAME: J_NAME TYPE:_CASE TYPE ABBREVIATION:_YR FILED:_
LN  NTY   NAME 1     NTY ABR  NAME 2          CASE-NO   TYPE  CCR
01  DF    KIRK, P     PL      FREED BLDG.     0920636   NOT   280
02  DF    KIRK, P     PL      NAT'L BANK/WA   8911690   INJ   281
03  DF    KIRK, P     PL      CA. PLANT PRO.  8849341   SWA   234
04  DF    KIRK, P     PL      MORROW, W.R.    8829923   NOT   165
05  WP    KIRK, P                             8821904   NOT   125
06  DF    KIRK, P     PL      SIB INT'L.      8821904   DEC   190
07  DF    KIRK, P     PL      GRISEBAUM, J.   8811334   NOT   281
08  DF    KIRK, P     PL      FIRST NAT'L BNK 8758508   AGR   280
09  DF    KIRK, P     PL      CITY PARTNERSHP.8752305   NOT   125
10  DF    KIRK, P     PL      HOME SVGS. ASSOC 8743933  NOT   164
11  DF    KIRK, P     PL      HOME SVGS. ASSOC 8742695  NOT   280
12  DF    KIRK, P     PL      MORROW, W.R     8731271   NOT   290
13  DF    KIRK, P     PL      LOCKWOOD, A & N 8730305   SWA   215
        M320D0078928636  00199 M320D0078911690   00399 M320D00788493

PRESS ENTER FOR NEXT PAGE * PRESS CLEAR TO TERMINATE * LINE-
NO + C + ENTER TO DCNI * LINE-NO + PF1 STO DCRI
=N                    CIVIL NAME INQUIRY      *DCQY* PAGE 2
LAST NAME: KIRK_____  FIRST NAME: PAUL_____
MIDDLE NAME: J___NAME TYPE:___CASE TYPE ABR:___YEAR FILED:__
LN  NTY   NAME 1     NTY ABR  NAME 2          CASE-NO   TYPE  CCR
01  DF    KIRK, P     PL      MANHATTAN CONST.9730277   AGR   125
02  DF    KIRK, P     PL      INTERFIRST BANK 8719281   NOT   281
03  DF    KIRK, P     PL      HARRIS CTY BANK 8716515   NOT   333
04  DF    KIRK, P     PL      RODEWAY INNS    8703746   AGR   164
05  DF    KIRK, P     PL      BANCTEXAS       8651234   NOT   295
06  DF    KIRK, P     PL      DEMONTROND BUI  8640955   LEA   280
07  DF    KIRK, P     PL      INTERFIRST BANK 8630858   NOT   130
08  DF    KIRK, P     PL      FIRST NAT'L BAN 8623819   NOT   125
09  DF    KIRK, P     PL      PAUL E WISE CO  8616107   NOT   333
10  DF    KIRK, P     PL      UNIV. STATE BAN 8515446   NOT   295
11  WP    KIRK, P                             8536549   DET   055
12  PL    KIRK, P     DF      COLUMBETTI, N   7953797   OTH   129
13  DF    KIRK, P     PL      CITY OF HOUSTON 8947617   TAX   189
      M320D0078730277   00199  M320D0078719281   00199  M320D0078765
```

CIVIL COURT RECORDS PROVIDE PERSONAL AND FINANCIAL INFORMATION NOT FOUND IN ANY SOURCES.

and dealings that are the basis of the lawsuit. Through these records, investigators often find bank accounts and lists of inventory and equipment, as well as tax returns and financial statements included in the depositions taken by the attorneys seeking to discover financial information in these suits.

3. *Personal injury or damages lawsuits* will often reveal the extent or nature of injuries suffered by an individual and can frequently uncover a history of prior claims made through employers or made against other individuals. By researching the settlements awarded or determining if his or her subject is suing to obtain such an award, the investigator can often discover assets made through insurance proceeds or previous employers that are self-insured, paying damages directly to a claimant.

BANKRUPTCY

In recent years, a greater number of people have filed personal or business bankruptcy to avoid their debts and financial obligations. The stigma of having declared bankruptcy has eroded to the point where today, many people think that bankruptcy is "in" and that by going through a bankruptcy they can avoid their liabilities and hide their assets from their creditors.

In conducting a search of bankruptcy records, the investigator should first obtain a copy of the bankruptcy petition filed by the debtor and the schedules of creditors, the parties who are owed money by the bankrupted party, as well as the list of assets filed by the debtor with the court. From the list of creditors, we determine the names of parties that extended credit to the debtor, parties that often have financial statements that reflect the assets held by their subjects at the time they established a relationship with that creditor.

By comparing the oldest financial statements against the newest financial statements filed either with your client or with the bankruptcy court, the investigator can look for the assets or items that were filed on the old financial statements and do not appear on the statements prepared most recently. These are the assets that the investigator should most closely examine. Through tracing the assets deleted from the oldest financial statements, we often find the transfers made to the spouse's maiden name, to children's trusts, or to third parties who hold these assets secretly for the debtor. If the investigator can establish the relationship with the new owner of the asset and prove that the transfer of assets was not an arm's length transaction, then the sale or transfer of these assets can be frequently overturned and the assets returned to the creditors.

Another interesting item to look for is the valuation of assets in a bankruptcy matter. Investigators have frequently found that household goods and personal items were listed in a bankruptcy at a very low rate and later claimed at a substantially higher rate (often 500 percent more) in an insurance loss or fire.

Once the information found in litigation records is added to the previously discovered personal information, the investigator is ready to search for tangible assets. These assets may include bank accounts, insurance policies, real estate, oil and gas interests, and other assets acquired through inheritance. The records of each of these transactions are found in the county courthouse.

REAL PROPERTY

Real property or deed records list the property transactions recorded between individuals or business entities in their jurisdiction. These records will document the legal description of real estate transferred from one party to any other party that acquires title to this property.

These records will frequently reflect the purchase or sale price, the mortgage obtained by the new property purchaser, and the cash or second mortgage acquired by the seller of the property. As stated above, these records will also reflect property transfers to other family members, trust entities created by the subject, or controlled business entities that are created to diminish the value of the assets or create a false transfer of the assets themselves.

The history of property transactions is determined by researching both the records of the county tax assessor and the county recorder. The tax assessor records the name of the taxpayer making payment on a given property and provides a determination of the value of the property by its tax assessment. The investigator should note that the tax assessor does not always value properties at 100 percent of their true value and should question the assessor's office about the valuation of properties in their jurisdiction.

The county recorder is the repository for records detailing the purchase, sale, foreclosure, or transfer of any properties in their county and is the office in which any party records a lien against assets owned by an individual. Investigators will find not only the record of properties bought and sold by their subjects, they may also find liens filed by the Internal Revenue Service for nonpayment of taxes or mechanics liens filed by companies doing home improvements or pool construction in these records. Since real estate is often coal, or other minerals found in the surrounding area.

PROBATE RECORDS

These record the distribution of assets to heirs through the wills of people filed in that county. These records list the deceased party, the heirs, and the full assets and liabilities of the deceased's estate as well as the distribution of the estate to the heirs. These records are usually very complete and detailed and list the bank accounts, certificates of deposit, insurance policies, personal effects, real estate holdings, and any other assets or liabilities in the deceased's estate. If the investigator discovers the existence of a will being probated, he or she can alert the client to file a claim in that probate and recover the debt before any assets are distributed to heirs. Like a bankruptcy, a probate lists both the assets and liabilities of the deceased and provides for the payment of liabilities before any assets are distributed.

UNIFORM COMMERCIAL CODE RECORDS

Also known as financing statements in some counties, uniform commercial code records are public filings made by creditors to record obligations against assets that they lend against, such as real estate, equipment, cattle, or other tangible items. These records are filed to document the existence of a loan made by a lender and to serve notice on other parties that the lender holds a secured interest in the assets pledged by a borrower.

By searching the UCC records, the investigator may find the name of the new bank used by the borrower or an undisclosed bank that the subject had pledged assets already secured by loans to the client. A search of these records may also lead to the discovery of other assets

UCC RECORDS, ALSO KNOWN AS FINANCING STATEMENTS, DOCUMENT THE EXISTENCE OF LOANS AND CAN LEAD INVESTIGATORS TO PREVIOUSLY UNKNOWN ASSETS OF THE SUBJECT.

the most valuable asset owned by many individuals, the investigators should thoroughly familiarize themselves with the type of transactions recorded and should be well versed in the terms used in these transactions.

OIL, GAS, AND MINERAL INTERESTS

These are filed in county recorder offices to document the ownership of oil, gas, and mineral leases obtained from parties who own the land on which these assets are found. The value of these assets will depend on the amount of oil or natural gas pumped out of the property or the amount of gold, silver, copper,

```
INTERTECT, INC. - 5300 MEMORIAL DR. #450, HOUSTON, TX. 77007
Phone 713/880-1111                                    Fax 713/880-2805
┌─────────────────────────────────────────────────────────────────┐
│                      LEVEL I ASSET REPORT                         │
│  CASE # _____ SUBJECT _____ │
│                                                                   │
│  DATE IN __/__/__  DATE OUT __/__/__  INVESTIGATOR _____   │
│  PERSONAL HISTORY                                                 │
│              FULL NAME _____  │
│  ADDRESS _____  │
│                                                                   │
│  DOB _____ SS# _____ SPOUSE _____   │
│                                              Voter Reg / Marriage │
│  BUSINESS HISTORY                                                 │
│  CORPORATIONS _____  │
│  _____   │
│  UCC _____   │
│  _____   │
│                                                                   │
│  LITIGATION HISTORY                                               │
│  CIVIL - SMALL CLAIMS _____    │
│          SUPERIOR _____    │
│          FEDERAL _____    │
│          BANKRUPTCY _____    │
│  LIENS / JUDGMENTS _____    │
│  CRIMINAL (if requested)                                          │
│  TAX ASSESSOR _____     │
│  REAL PROPERTY _____     │
│  _____     │
│  PROBATE _____     │
│  BANKING _____     │
│  INVESTIGATIVE DISCOVERY                                          │
│  _____   │
│  _____   │
│  _____   │
│  _____   │
└─────────────────────────────────────────────────────────────────┘
```

A SAMPLE COPY OF INTERTECT'S LEVEL I ASSET REPORT.

such as cattle or crops raised on farm land, business inventories or equipment owned by the subject, or the existence of otherwise unrecorded business contracts that were pledged to secure a loan or credit line.

Once the investigator has examined all of the above sources in a given county, the information should be collated in a report that lists the material found in each of these sources. While examining these records, the investigator should look for references to activities or transactions in other counties that may lead to the discovery of activities or assets in those areas. If a search in one county provides a record of assets secured in another county or state, the investigator should then consider conducting a search of the full range of public record filings conducted in the first jurisdiction searched.

A search of the second jurisdiction may lead to a third or fourth area of search, each adding to the assets of the subject being investigated. Once a full picture of the activities and financial interests of the subject is put together, then the investigator is ready to turn the report over to the client, who can then use this information to ask further questions and discover more information from the material compiled by the investigator.

CHAPTER 12

Tracking Down the Global Criminal

atching today's sophisticated white-collar criminal is like peeling an onion, where you have to go through his or her activities layer by layer, ring by ring, to get to the core of the matter. The modern-day music man, unlike those of the movies, cannot outrun his past by traveling from city to city ahead of his bad news.

Today's computer technology and on-line information services provide instant access to information throughout the United States and gives businessmen and investigators the key to their pasts with the press of a button (of course, you need a computer, modem, and subscription to an on-line newspaper service). Our new world-class con man now has to create complex corporate identities and offshore banking relationships to "muddy the waters" through a web of complex maneuvers designed to hide his true identity and the ultimate destination of his ill-gotten goods. When you do business with those people who appear to have "all the flash, but none of the cash," beware! Those that sound too good to be true almost always are.

When conducting an investigation into the activities, business dealings, and assets of a person doing business in foreign countries or believed to have hidden assets outside the United States, the investigator has to gather information from a variety of sources. To be successful in conducting foreign asset investigations, the investigator must do the following:

- Document the foreign travel of the subject to a specific country
- Determine the activities of the subject conducted in a foreign country
- Discover the location of bank accounts and business relationships of the subject that relate to that country

• Locate and interview the parties having access to this information

There are a number of resources available to investigators to determine if an individual has traveled to a foreign country. The most widely known resource, available to police agencies, is a data base developed and maintained by U.S. Customs known as EPIC, or the El Paso Intelligence Center (as discussed briefly in Chapter 6). This data base collates and records the reentry of each person into the United States from a foreign port.

By recording the information on a U.S. Customs Form that documents the reentry point and goods purchased and declared to Customs, the investigator can use this data base to document the frequent foreign travel of parties believed to be involved in drug smuggling, money laundering, or other crimes investigated by the U.S. Customs Office and other investigative agencies. The information in EPIC is reported to the Financial Crimes Enforcement Network (FinCen, see Chapter 6), headquartered in Washington, D.C. FinCen provides this information to law enforcement and regulatory agencies interested in determining the travel history and patterns of parties under examination by state and federal agencies investigating drug, financial, regulatory, or organized crime matters. Investigators have found a number of ways to determine the existence of foreign travel by a person suspected of going to another country. Some of these methods include:

1. When a suspect is arrested for any reason, a thorough search of his or her person and luggage should be conducted to determine if the individual is carrying a passport or documents indicating his or her foreign travel or business activities. If a passport or other records are found, investigators should copy the pages recording foreign passport stamps and visas. While searching the subject, investigators should also look for receipts and matchbooks from foreign hotels. This will lead you to the place the suspect stayed and the telephone charges made from that room to local lawyers, banks, and business contacts in that country.

2. One of the easiest ways to determine the foreign business activities of an individual is to examine the business, personal, and mobile telephone records of the subject to identify countries and parties that the subject has called overseas. These records will often lead to a bank, attorney, or business agent that the investigated subject has contacted to set up a business or financial relationship in a foreign location. In either a criminal or a civil case, telephone records can be subpoenaed to establish and document the telephone toll record of the person being investigated.

3. Another valuable source of information for determining foreign travel is the credit card statements of the subject. These records will often reveal a detailed account of the airline ticket purchase, hotel accommodations, and purchases made by the subject in the foreign country in which he or she travels.

Investigators traced a man suspected of embezzling $12 million, a Colombian economic ministry attache, by tracking his American Express charges from Colombia to the United States and then to Austria. Through working with the credit card security department, investigators were able to document the daily financial, business, and travel activities of the attache and were able to maintain surveillance on his movements through the hotel reservations and restaurant charges made to his account. This information provided a detailed history of the attache's activities during the period of time crucial to the investigation and helped to place him in locations where bank accounts were ultimately located through investigation at banks in the town identified by these records. (Did you know that many European banks secretly photograph and record the identity of every individual entering their banks? Well, you do now.)

4. While checking the record of banking transactions, the investigator should also look for information concerning the purchase of traveler's checks, money orders, wire transfers, or overnight packages billed to the subject's account. Through the discovery of these instruments, investigators can determine the location where money orders or traveler's checks were cashed, which may be the same

location or bank where the subject opened an account. The ultimate destination of wire transfers, telexes, or overnight packages may also be the financial institution, attorney, or agent with whom the subject set up his foreign business activities.

5. If the investigator is unsuccessful in determining the location of foreign accounts by tracing the transactions, then the next step is to locate the people who had knowledge of the personal and business activities of the subject, to include enemies, friends, and former employees who have information pertinent to his activities.

Very often, a business executive's secretary makes his or her travel plans, often through a travel agent. Both of these people may be able to contribute reliable information to the investigator. Another possible resource is a companion who accompanied the subject for recreational purposes on a trip, particularly when the destination is Bermuda, the Bahamas, the Cayman Islands, or a similar tropical financial haven.

In one case, a secretary informed investigators that her former employer was secretly sending money out of the country through his attorney. The secretary gave specific details of the dates and times of the foreign travel, the information was transmitted to U.S. Customs, and the attorney was arrested when he attempted to leave the United States without declaring cash in excess of the $10,000 allowance required by law. (It's not illegal to carry more money outside the United States, but it must be declared to U.S. Customs or it's subject to forfeiture under Title 21 US CODE.)

Once he was searched and his money confiscated, the attorney realized that he had a choice to either state that the money was his and face income tax evasion charges for unreported income or admit that he was acting as an agent for another party and face the lesser charge of illegally transporting money out of the United States, which would probably be dismissed if he cooperated on the case against his client. (Guess what he did?)

How do you find the secretary or travel agent who books the trips for your suspect? The secretary is most likely the person who notarized the subject's business documents. Look at the letters, legal documents, and other financial documents executed by the subject and then call the state notary board to determine the current registered address and bonding agent of the secretary/notary who once worked for your subject. As the person responsible for filing, recording, and notarizing company records, a corporate secretary often feels the responsibility of illegal activities being conducted by her employer and will seek to protect herself from future litigation by keeping a personal diary or copies of documents that she feels may compromise her position if her boss' scheme has been found out.

Since they are often the ones signing checks, and therefore liable for the activities perpetrated through these checks (according to IRS and tax court decisions), many secretaries feel either a natural hesitancy to sign such documents or, when forced to prepare and sign these, keep their own records to protect themselves in case of future problems with the law. In the course of an ongoing offshore investigation, investigators should question the secretary or executive assistant of the subject and determine if she has the following information:

- Personal diary calendar or daytimer that details her employer's travel and business activities

- Personal Rolodex of numbers frequently called for her employer

- Notary log that records documents that she notarized

- Telephone directories that she kept to remember key contacts of her employer, especially in other cities or countries

- Copies of documents made because of her personal concerns about the ethics or business activities in which she was involved or her employers made her sign

To locate the travel agent, first try the Rolodex of the subject or his secretary, if it is available to you. Every businessman has a favorite travel agent and usually stays with him or her for years. If there is a travel agency in your subject's office building, or one in close proximity to the office, give it a call and see if your subject or his company had an account with it. If so, there is a good chance that the agency will have at least a three-year history of the travel records of your subject and can tell you exactly where and how often her or she traveled, both domestically and internationally, and where he or she stayed, if booked in a hotel.

If you can't find the travel agent, then it is time to search the records of the Airline Reporting Corporation (ARC) in Washington, D.C., which is the clearinghouse for domestic airline tickets of all the major air carriers. ARC compiles and collates all domestic U.S. air tickets, and its sister organization, International Air Transport Association (IATA, headquartered in Montreal Quebec, Canada, 2000 Peal St., H3A 2RH), collates the records of foreign travel for many of the world's airlines. The records of ARC and IATA can help you determine the name and location of the travel agency used by your subject, which can lead you to the cities and countries in which the subject has traveled. Many offshore investigations begin through information provided by fired secretaries, spurned spouses, or disgruntled employees who harbor a grudge against the wealth or illegal activities of someone they know. The records they keep often provide the missing link necessary to prove the existence of foreign banking relationships or hidden business interests.

Sheila was the secretary and part-time lover of one of the nation's largest pornography dealers and served him faithfully for over 12 years. As his confidant and bookkeeper, she traveled with him on his Carribean vacations and helped him set up several Cayman Islands bank accounts in which she deposited money, to the tune of $5 million over the course of her employment and relationship. Sheila took half of all cash receipts made in her employer's business and converted the proceeds to cashier's checks and money orders

and then sent these deposits to her employer's sister in Canada. The sister in turn put these envelopes in an overnight package and forwarded them to the Cayman Islands Bank so that no trail to the Cayman Islands could be linked directly to her brother.

Through the years as Sheila gained weight and became less attractive, her employer entered the middle-aged crazies and became obsessed with younger women. First he started dating topless dancers and then brought a younger secretary into his organization, a women whom Sheila saw as a threat and who ultimately took over Sheila's relationship with her boss as well as her bookkeeping position. Her boss, oblivious to anything but sex and drugs, did not consider Sheila a threat and threw her away just as easily as a child grows up and throws away their favorite doll.

Forced to go out into the job market and unable to find a job anywhere near the money she was making for the pornographer, Sheila became very bitter. In her anger, she became a willing witness when she was approached by our investigator and an Internal Revenue Service agent investigating tax matters in the pornography business. Sheila provided oral testimony about the trips to the Cayman Islands and the existence of Cayman Islands bank accounts in the pornographer's mother's maiden name. She produced copies of deposits and overnight package receipts documenting payments made into the Cayman Island accounts set up to hide the money made from the book business and drugs sold by her former employer.

With this evidence, the government agent was able to document not only income tax fraud but income from dealing in drugs, which gave the U.S. Attorney sufficient grounds to obtain an indictment and conviction against the pornographer and his business by obtaining the Cayman Islands banking records through an multilateral assistance treaty (MLAT) request.

Once we have established the existence of foreign travel on a subject being investigated, the next order of business is to determine where the subject stayed in the foreign country and what business activities were conducted by the subject while there. One of the best sources for developing information of this type is the credit card activity of the subject under investigation. The ease and convenience of credit card usage works to the advantage of the investigator. The majority of people who travel overseas charge their hotel bills on credit cards so that they don't have to purchase or exchange foreign currency or worry about the foreign rate of exchange. (Have you ever tried to figure out pesos to dollars?)

The major credit card companies quickly and conveniently solve this problem by accepting all major currencies, but create a new problem for the subject because they efficiently document the date and place that their owner stayed while in that foreign country. By locating the hotel used by the subject, investigators can determine the names of people and identities of businesses or agents that the subject contacted through an examination of the telephone records billed to the subject's account from the hotel.

An examination of a telephone record detail of a hotel bill helped determine the existence of foreign bank accounts and the names of business agents used by an executive alleged to have transferred millions of dollars from a Texas Savings & Loan. Through the examination of credit card records, investigators determined that the executive stayed at a hotel in Berne, Switzerland, and while at the hotel, made telephone calls to two banks, an attorney, and a foreign private postal service located in that town.

By examining the photographs made daily of the parties entering the Swiss banks called by the subject, investigators were able to document that the executive visited a certain bank on a specific date and opened accounts with the proceeds transferred from his savings and loan through a series of financial transactions to his Swiss bank.

The phone calls found to have been made during these hotel visits were a crucial piece of evidence in establishing a link between the executive and a Swiss attorney with whom he did business. The attorney made purchases of real property in the United States for the bene-fit of the executive, who claimed that he was only the caretaker of these properties. By proving the existence of prior conversations brtween the executive and the attorney, government regulators were able to establish a relationship between the two and seize properties purchased for the executive's benefit in the United States and prove a conspiracy on the part of the two parties.

In addition to examining the credit card statements of persons suspected of foreign travel, investigators should look for the purchase of money orders or traveler's checks, instruments that are also frequently used to make foreign purchases and pay for expenses incurred while traveling out of country. A careful examination of traveler's checks and money orders will disclose the same type of information as credit cards such as hotel accommodations, travel within the foreign country, restaurants, shops, and banks that cash these instruments for the benefit of the traveler.

Examination and analysis of instruments of this type may indicate the location of new bank accounts, the leasing of safety deposit boxes, and the purchase of extravagant presents or gifts such as diamonds, jewelry, and expensive watches. In several cases, investigators have even traced purchases of expensive foreign automobiles through the purchase of traveler's checks bought by the subject in the United States.

An important step in an investigation of this type is to determine if the subject has traveled overseas personally, or has that subject sent an outside party, such as his accountant, attorney, or another family member out of the country with the assets he or she is attempting to hide. An accountant, representing a number of doctors in a suburban metropolitan area, conceived a scheme to take the unreported income made by his clients to the Cayman Islands where it was deposited in numbered accounts in the doctor's name. For years, the accountant made a trip every month, the first weekend after the end of each month, to the Cayman Islands, complete with diving gear and scuba tanks.

The creative accountant gathered up the

FREQUENT TRIPS TO THE CAYMAN ISLANDS MAY ALERT IRS OR CUSTOMS AGENTS TO SOME ILLEGAL FINANCIAL TRANSACTIONS—OR THEY MAY TIP OFF A SAVVY PRIVATE INVESTIGATOR.

who had given him the money to deposit in the Cayman Islands.

BAGGING THE TRASH

Sometimes, the best evidence in the investigation of offshore matters comes from getting down and dirty, that is, bagging your subject's trash. Investigators have long known that the garbage thrown away by subjects being investigated may contain a variety of clues and evidence.

This evidence could include envelopes that list a return address from parties having knowledge of the suspect, the address of foreign banks and correspondence, confirmations from overnight packages sent overseas, or bank statements and checks that show the routing numbers and accounts where checks were cashed or funds were transferred through a suspect's bank to an offshore entity.

Most people throw away those handwritten notes scribbled in haste while picking up messages from their telephone recorder or those phone calls that come after they have gotten into bed. By conducting trash pulls on the subject's garbage, particularly at the end of the month, the lucky investigator may find documents that lead to offshore business activities or people that have knowledge of the information that can assist the investigator gain further knowledge into the activities of their subject.

There are certain days of the year, particularly holidays, that are magic to any investigator, days in which they know through years of experience that people will perform certain activities such as calling home to family and loved ones or sending them a card or note to show they care. These are the times that smart investigators focus on, particularly when bagging someone's trash, to determine who people really are, where they are, and what they are hiding from the rest of the world. On days

unreported cash of each of his clients at the end of the month, put the money in envelopes, and taped the money to the inside of his scuba tanks. This crime went unreported for years until the accountant's wife decided to file for divorce and turned her husband in for the reward on an income tax evasion scheme. In six years, he had illegally carried several millions of dollars past U.S. Customs and Cayman Islands Immigration by carrying it right before their very eyes, in the scuba tanks that he used as his excuse to go to the islands each month.

The IRS alerted U.S. Customs, who then monitored the flight plans of aircraft traveling to the Cayman Islands during his normal travel times. On his next flight, the accountant was detained and an inspection of his scuba tanks was conducted. When Custom's agents found more than $100,000 in his possession, he was charged with carrying more than $10,000 outside the United States without a Customs Declaration and a charge was made by the IRS relating to unreported income of the monies found. Facing the two charges, the accountant elected to plead guilty to the lesser charge of transporting money and gave the IRS an affidavit and testimony revealing the identity of the parties like this, people show their soul and investigators focus on these times and their families to sneak a peek into their private lives. What are these magic times?

• Valentine's Day. This is the day for lovers and the day to find someone's secret heart throb. Bag someone's trash after Valentine's Day and you find return addresses from envelopes sent to their mother, lover, or special friend. This is also a day to

INVESTIGATING IS SOMETIMES A DIRTY JOB; GOING THROUGH YOUR SUBJECT'S GARBAGE CAN PROVIDE CLUES OR EVIDENCE NOT READILY AVAILABLE ELSEWHERE.

their stuff, and many do, acting out their favorite fantasy and letting it all hang out. If you wonder what someone does when no one is looking, this is the night to find out.

check for receipts for flowers, perfume, or candy on the charge card to locate that special someone.

• Mother's Day. This is a day for mothers, and even the most hardened criminals may send their mothers a telephone call to let them know that they are still alive. This is a good day to run mother's phone bill and find her son who is hiding from the law.

• Father's Day. Not as many wise guys call home to dad, but it is still a smart day to check the trash and phone bills when looking for errant sons or daughters who can't be found any other way.

•Halloween. This is definitely the one night of the year that people show their true colors. This is the night for crazies to strut

• Thanksgiving. As a time of family gatherings, this is the time to put surveillance on your subject's family to see if he comes home for dinner. Who knows, you might even get your turkey.

• Christmas. This is the best time to check credit card receipts for gifts and purchases that don't make it home. It is also time to watch those special relationships developing among all the good cheer. Be sure to bag the trash because this is where the best cards and envelopes are found from people who only make contact once a year.

SUMMARY

There is no one miracle way to make an offshore investigation. Cases of this type are made by hitting all the bases and chasing down every possible lead in the investigator's bag of tricks. The resources that we have discussed here, if diligently pursued, will lead to the discovery of evidence, if it is there, in many of your most complex cases. As investigators, we are all seeking to expand our knowledge in this area and look for new ways to get an edge on the wise guys.

CHAPTER 13

Getting to Know You

ne evening as I sat behind my desk after a long day's work, a reporter from the *New York Times* called our office and asked what was new in the investigative business, what was going on that he could make a human interest story of for his next deadline.

The first thing that popped into my head was the rise in numbers of background checks in cases where we have been hired to check out the background and assets of potential spouses.

"You see," I told the reporter, "women are now waiting longer to get married, into their 30s and 40s, and have accumulated a little piece of the rock themselves. They don't want to make the same mistakes that their friends and parents made, go through two or three divorces and end up broke in their 50s with their looks and beauty gone. They want to marry someone equally, if not more, successful and find someone without any financial baggage or a poor track record of his own."

The reporter was fascinated. Here was technology at work, doing something that people could really care about and relate to, finding a new spouse. The rest was history. The article appeared on the front page of the Sunday *New York Times*, the most widely read paper in the country. The story was picked up by the Associated Press and United Press International and run in many other newspapers throughout the world.

The minute the paper hit the street, my phone went crazy. My answering service called in a panic and asked, "Mr. P, what have you done?" Donahue was on one line, Geraldo on another, and Joan Rivers said she was a personal friend! All of them wanted me on their shows, with one of my potential husband hunters, the next day.

Out of the blue, this story created a whole new area of business for PIs all over the country. Dating detectives started advertising in singles magazines and lonely hearts columns, offering their sleuthing abilities to discover unadmitted prior divorces, current spouses, and to disprove or verify the financial status of the new love that "was just too good to be true."

Within weeks, our volume of "Love Dick" cases (that what the article in *Playboy* called us) grew from one or two a week to five a day. At $500 a pop, that's a fine little side business. Little did I know that this human interest interview would strike such a chord and create a big time business opportunity for investigators everywhere.

The work itself is simple. The same search conducted to check out debtors for banks is ideal for sniffing out potential spouses, only you give it a new spin. A voter and marriage search verify the name and address; litigation records find the ex-spouses, tax liens, judgments, and debts; and real property and probate document the assets. No problem, man! If the client wants to know where the prospective spouse goes on Friday nights, then check parking tickets and, as a last resort, follow him by surveillance.

What have we found? Three out of four prospects investigated are not what they claimed to be. Now, we only get the ones that already have created some suspicion, but that's a pretty good average. Most of the men we searched had more wives than they admitted to. Half of them were still married some-

where else, and four were real serious nutso cases, sociopaths who were deep into pain and suffering. One turned out to be a serial killer; he just hadn't been caught yet and still isn't in jail because we can't find his victims.

If you want a piece of this business, send a flyer announcing your service out to the dating clubs (offer to do the background through them for a 20-percent referral fee), consider a small ad in the personals column of the local newspapers that cater to dating, and go out Friday nights to the mating dances, sponsored by social networking clubs in your town. Chances are, once you get to meet the crowd, you'll be asked to give a short seminar on the dangers of dating or the "red flags" that indicate deception in the social scene.

If you don't already know these red flags, here they are, compliments of E.J. Pankau:

- Hair gets longer.

- Clothes get flashier.

- Changes cologne.

- Boxer shorts become bikini underwear.

- Joins a health club.

- Starts a diet.

Investigation Simplified

fter watching all the TV and movie detective shows, everybody thinks that cases are solved by a snitching informant or a Sherlock Holmes-type rocket scientist who weaves his way through the many convolutions concocted by the perpetrator of crime. Every case we see takes bizarre twists and turns, with layer after layer of plots and intrigue where we search for mysterious and elusive clues.

Anyone who has been in the detective business for a while and has been at least moderately successful knows that every case has its own pattern and flow. It has a structure and set of parameters that have to be in place for the crime to have been committed or for the case to exist. Each case has a beginning and an end, both of which are usually known or discovered at the onset of the investigation. The best investigators are those who work both ends of the case, toward the middle. That is, they take the facts known from the crime scene and work backward through the incidents that led to the crime, but they also gather facts known before the crime and work forward through the commission of the crime, until both ends meet in the middle. Working in this fashion fills in most of the blanks and tells the who, what, when, where, and why of most cases.

What does this mean to you, the investigator? It means that there is a body of knowledge, a set of facts and circumstances, a profile of each type of crime, that show how these same crimes have been committed, over and over again. You see, there are no new crimes, only new ways of doing them. If you want to look, most of them are laid out in the bible, etched in stone when Moses brought them down from the mountain. The following cases are simplified in the extreme but give you some idea of the profile of each of these kinds of cases.

HOMICIDE OR MURDER

In the great majority of these cases, we start with a body found dead or missing. The dead body is usually alive with clues, so that is our first area of investigation: what is the physical evidence, were there signs of violence, was the death caused by friend or foe (90 percent of all murders are done by people who know the victim).

Years ago, the sons of the two wealthiest ranchers in south Texas fought over a girlfriend, starting with their fists and ending with .44 Magnum pistols. There were no witnesses to the shooting except the girlfriend, and her story changed every day. She started saying what a wonderful boyfriend the deceased was, and how he'd never harm a fly, until we found the maintenance man who patched up the 12 bullet holes in the roof of her apartment, made when the boyfriend got drunk and shot up her ceiling on more than one occasion. The testimony of the maintenance man, combined with the blood/alcohol count of both parties, confirmed the story of the accused killer and resulted in a lesser charge of involuntary manslaughter rather than the premeditated murder asked for by the prosecutor.

Once the physical evidence and crime scene are evaluated, the investigator goes back to when the deceased was alive and determines who his friends were, who his enemies were, and if anyone had a motive for the crime. Included in motive is why the person was killed, for love, hate, or money. Once the physical evidence and motive establish certain facts, the investigator then ties the suspects to the crime, throwing out the ones who don't fit for reasons of alibi, motive, and evidence. The focus narrows on the suspects with the most motive and clearest evidence until a conclusion is reached.

ASSET SEARCH

The search for people and their money is the fastest-growing area of investigative business in America. More and more people are skipping out on their debts and flocking to yellow page advertising lawyers who promise to make them financially bulletproof and invulnerable to their creditors' claims. In an investigation of this type, the keys to a successful investigation are as follows:

1. Identify the subject.
2. Determine their business entities.
3. Trace their real property and tangible assets through public records and online information sources.
4. Interview the former spouse, creditors, business associates, and former friends who were also left holding the bag.

DOMESTIC CASES

Everybody has a pattern, particularly when living with or married to a partner. The first step is to find the change in the pattern which tells you when a new partner or relationship entered into the picture.

1. When did he start changing cologne, clothes, or switch from boxer shorts to bikini underwear?
2. What's his current daily travel pattern?
3. Where are the holes in the travel pattern where he can't account for his time?
4. Whom does he call? (Check those mobile phone records.)

Follow up with targeted surveillance during unaccountable times. Through the conduct of thousands of divorce cases, I have found three main areas of investigation common to these matters: background, financial, and child custody investigations. Each of these investigations has a specific goal and requires the proof of different facts. The purpose of the background investigation is to determine the prior life history and past activities of your subject, to prove that these activities of the past have continued and bear a strong relationship to the current activities and probable future activities of this person (examples include alcoholism, child abuse, molestation, etc.).

Knowing a divorce is somewhere in their future, many wealthy individuals hide their assets and create a plan to minimize their wealth, often years before a divorce. These people may also create a number of artificial debts that diminish their estates or devalue companies and business that they plan to build up once the divorce is final and the companies are back in their hands.

Perhaps the most hotly contested aspect of domestic relation investigations, and certainly the most emotionally trying, is the fight for child custody. Over the years, many investigators have been used (often very successfully) to present and document the evidence as to the fitness and capabilities of spousal parents and one side or the other's ability to care for the future needs of their children. Investigators are frequently used in this area to "paint a picture" of the true living conditions of a parent and their children, to show how this parent's relationship with the child is in the present and can be projected into the future.

The investigator's job is to document the daily routine of the parents and the children to show the degree of supervisory care on the part of each parent and to verify any outside harmful influences that would be against the best interests of the child. Frequently, investigators are called in to create a "day in the life movie" showing the children with their client and how the child benefits from the attention and care provided in their home. In presenting a case of this type to a judge or jury, it's critical that the attorney, investigator, and client document every potential area of differences and conflicts between the parents so that they can show circumstances that the judge or jury can personally relate to. Everyone has different values and will attach a certain weight to particular issues, evaluating their decision on their own experience and things they perceive to be in the best interests of the children.

A good example of this is shown in one of my very first cases. In one of our most highly contested custody cases, the wife was having a relationship outside of the marriage. The husband, trying to get custody of his two young children, claimed the relationship of his spouse with the new boyfriend was "detrimental and dangerous" to the children and

asked for a jury trial. In proving the facts of this case, we first introduced evidence to the jury detailing the various meetings of the spouse and her lover and established that she was living and sleeping with another man in the presence of her children. To this issue, the judge didn't blink an eye.

Our investigator then produced evidence, taken from the garbage cans in the spouse's home, documenting drug usage through evidence found in the trash. Again, we received no indication of interest from the judge.

What finally moved both the judge and jury was a photograph of two 6-foot boa constrictors that were kept in the bedroom of the wife's new home. These snakes were the property of the lover and were both large enough to hurt the children and were particularly offensive to several members of the jury. One of my greatest moments in court was when the judge leaned over the bench and looked at me with bugged-out eyes, asking, "How big were them snakes?"

In cases where both parents could be regarded as equally fit by jurors, then the investigator's job is to show that his client would be at least as fit, if not more so, to care for the children and to see to their future welfare. A creative and diligent investigator will look further for those witnesses that can testify to the specific growth needs of the children that can best be provided by his client. In many cases, jurors will particularly relate to male children where witnesses, such as scout leaders and sports coaches, are corralled to testify as to the athletic ability of the child and his father, where female children would be more closely related to witnesses having knowledge of the creativity and artistic inclination issues, such as music and dance. In close cases, these issues will often be the determining factor in custody issues.

PERSONAL INJURY

In life, health, disability, or worker's comp claims, you follow the trail of their activities.

1. How and under what circumstances were they injured, damaged, or affected?

2. Where are they now (and what are they doing)?
3. Make their day (or their night) by surveillance of their activities.
4. Check the record and see if they have a history of previous claims. Several states are now passing laws requiring that insurance companies create or use the services of a Special Investigative Unit (SIU) to investigate claims in their states. This SIU rule can be a bonanza to private investigators, as many insurance companies don't have the man power or the financial ability to maintain an SIU in every state and will therefore have to look for private investigators with skills in this area. One of the best things you can do is learn more about the International Association of Special Investigative Units (address in Baltimore, Maryland) and determine if your state already has or is developing its own chapter.

TRADEMARK FRAUD

The biggest case I ever investigated (as far as fee goes) was chasing down those heinous criminals who copied or altered Spud McKenzie's appearance on T-shirts, hats, and similar materials. To find trademark fraud, you should:

1. Locate the phony merchandise (street corners, flea markets, and trade fairs are your most likely candidates).
2. Work up the chain by becoming a seller. Once you buy products from a vendor once or twice, ask him where he got them so that you can become a dealer to.
3. Find the distributor and bag his trash to get the shipping labels from cartons that were thrown out. Every kind of investigation has its own set of rules and its own means of investigation. The more cases you do in any area, the better you get at them because you learn how they have had to been done in order to work. If you're ever stuck on an investigation, call one of your associates, or any other investigator you trust, and run the ideas by him. He may be able to help by giving you new ideas that you haven't thought of.

Many years ago, one of my friendly neighborhood competitors got a big case from a client who was a little too much for him to handle. The client's wife, after several years of a bad marriage, took off one day with her husband's gold coin collection, worth over $300,000, and headed for parts unknown. Neither the investigator nor the client had any idea where she went, but Joe's fee was to be one-third of recovery, once his client put his hands on the money and his wife (he didn't want the wife, just the money). After working the case for more than 24 hours with no clues at all, Joe called me and asked if I could help him to determine where she had gone.

His offer of a split of the recovery was the best I'd had that day, so we went over all of the information the client provided and then looked over the house just to see if I could think of any new ideas. Pulling up into the driveway, I saw some heavy marks, that looked to be tire tracks, leading from the driveway to the back bedroom door, which is where most of the gold and personal things that the wife took, came from. Something clicked in my mind and my mouth rolled out, "U-Haul, they had to have a trailer." The stuff was too heavy, they had to have a trailer. The client and another detective thought about this approximately two seconds, then the light bulb went on in their heads too.

I told the client to get me her photo while we drew up a reward poster and made a hundred copies at the nearest Kwik Kopy. We took those posters to every trailer dealer in town and finally found the one we were looking for, the one who rented our sweet little lady a trailer from Houston to Denver. Why did he help us? Could it have been the $1,000 reward on the wanted poster, or just his civic duty? Yes, he took the bucks.

One of our investigators flew immediately to Denver while the other collected the client. We all arrived at the Denver U-Haul Center hours before the wife and had the pleasure of watching her drive up (with a new boyfriend) to turn in the trailer, which was now empty.

After that, it was a simple matter of following her back to the hotel and explaining to the new boyfriend that he might be an accessory to kidnapping and theft (you see, he'd just gotten out of jail a week before and met our sweet young lady in a kicker bar), which left our lady alone with her husband. After several hours of "I didn't mean it's," and "I love you's," the couple drove back to Houston together, and we collected our fee.

Surveillance Secrets

The secret of superior surveillance is to get all of the pertinent information available about the subject you are investigating before you ever begin to follow him or her. At the outset of any investigation, you need to determine everything you can about the driving habits and patterns of your subject, the places he or she frequents, and the kinds of things he likes to do. If your client has this information, it narrows your fields of inquiry substantially and lets you concentrate on what is already a difficult job, following someone through traffic when he or she knows the destination and you don't. Before you get in the car and rush off to follow someone, try to get the following information.

1. A history of the daily activities of your subject to include where he or she works, lives, goes for lunch, and frequents after work.
2. If your subject has a mobile phone, try to get (either through your client or your own sources) the mobile phone records of your subject. These telephone logs record both incoming and outgoing calls, local and long distance.

By analyzing the timing of the calls, especially by looking at who was called on the way to and from work, you can often find the name and address of the person who most occupies your subject's mind, namely the meaningful other. If you can't get car telephone records, either because the subject doesn't have one or your sources aren't that good, then try to determine if your subject goes out of town and stays in a particular hotel. One of the private investigators oldest tricks is to obtain the hotel telephone records of a person who goes out of town and feels bulletproof and invisible because no one knows him in Denver.

Through doing hundreds of these investigations, I've seen that most people eat dinner in the restaurant, have a few drinks in the bar, and then go up to their rooms and make two phone calls. The first call is to the honey and goes something like this: "I love you, I need you, I want you, and I'll see you tomorrow night." The second call, of course, is to the wife: "I'm beat, I'm whipped, I'm tired, I'll be home in three days."

You don't know how to get this phone bill? It's real easy! Just call the hotel the next week after your subject leaves and asks for the audit or bookkeeping department with this little white lie. "Hello, this is Bobby Johnson with the Audit Department of Intergalactic Industries. Our salesman, Mr. Smith, was in your hotel last week and made a number of long distance phone calls on his bill. He didn't itemize these in his expense account, and I need to get those numbers for verification that they were business related."

They'll give them to you every time. By having the information listed above, you will soon have a much better idea of the movement patterns and the people whom your subject is likely to see if you lose contact in traffic or have to break off surveillance because the subject is "starting to wag his tail." The first time I had to follow someone, my supervisor just told me to go out there and follow him to see where he was going.

My introduction to the art of following someone in the car was purely by trial and error, which I promise you is the worst way to learn. Unfortunately, there are no schools that teach auto surveillance, or I haven't found one. So most investigators learn by trial and error. There is nothing more discouraging than trying to follow someone day after day and losing him in traffic or feeling that he knows you are following him.

When I first worked for another investigator, before the ink was even dry on my pocket card, I was sent out to follow a husband whose wife thought he had a serious drinking problem. You see, the husband often came home late at night and couldn't really tell his wife where he had been; he just told his wife that he was confused and trying to work out his problems. (In hindsight, having done this business for many years, I would now know this was just an excuse and the husband's real problem was that he had one too many women.) The wife asked us to follow him and document the places he went and how much he drank so that she could help him confront his problems and get professional psychiatric help if he needed it.

The first five days, I followed him to work, stared at his office door for several hours, and then watched him go to lunch with clients or lose me in lunch-hour traffic. The afternoons were just as bad, sweating in a hot car, staring at every car that left his office complex, and fighting the urge to use that glass jar we all carry on surveillances. After work, Tom got on the five-lane freeway heading away from his house, and I lost him in a sea of cars, all trying to beat each other out of town.

On the sixth day, Tom went to one of the town's fanciest restaurants, ate lunch, and came out with a carryout bag. As soon as I saw that bag, my alarms sounded. Having done this myself, I intuitively knew what was going on. Tom was taking a lunch to a sick friend. I could almost see the grin on his face as he eased out of the parking lot, drove through the residential back streets of River Oaks, and pulled in to an upscale townhouse complex right off that same freeway that I had lost him on for the last five days. In a few minutes, Tom was inside the townhouse courtyard, knocking on the door of unit 14, and walking into the arms of one of the most beautiful women I've ever seen in my life.

When I laid out the real source of Tom's problems for his spouse, she was at first stunned and couldn't believe that her husband was actually seeing another woman. In fact, she felt that this couldn't be someone he was having an affair with and insisted on seeing the situation herself (if you've been in this business long enough, you'll see that this happens many times).

So on the next day I went to the townhouse complex, told the sales agent that I was interested in purchasing the townhouse across from our friends, and obtained a key so that I could bring my wife over after work and look at the color schemes to see if it would match with our furniture. As it got dark, my client and I sat in the vacant apartment and talked about the possible scenarios that wouldn't lead to infidelity. Maybe this was some sick employee or the wife of a friend who he was bringing lunch to. "Let's see," I said, and we continued to wait in the gathering darkness for Tom to appear.

First, a young couple came into the courtyard, then another single man, and then our boy Tom walked in, just like he owned the place (we later found out that he did). My client tensed, almost called out to him, and then dropped her jaw as a long-haired, buxom blonde woman in a negligee wrapped her arms around my client's husband as he entered the door not 20 feet from where we sat.

If I hadn't recognized the opportunity at the restaurant or had given up because I couldn't follow him in rush hour traffic, Tom would still be "doing his thing" today. These same surveillance techniques work on domestic, personal injury, or internal investigations.

Look for the unusual, for the changes in a person's pattern that don't belong, and focus your investigation where these situations lead. When following someone in a mobile surveillance, you literally have to drive the subject's car. By putting yourself in the driver's seat of the car that you're following, you know what lights you have to make. Surveillance is really an art and takes a touch or feel that helps you see where your driver is going and what they are going to do. Once you've followed someone to his ultimate location, then the hard part begins.

Now, you've got to determine what he is doing in there or, if they've gone to a hotel, what room he's in. The easy way is to do two-person surveillance with a driver and a walker. This way, you can follow your subjects in their car and drop off your walker so that they can maintain foot surveillance on your subjects and see precisely where they go. My choice for a walker is almost always a woman, preferably with a carry-on bag or shopping bag who can look the part, walk the walk, and talk the talk when she gets inside.

Unfortunately, on many occasions, surveillance is a one-man show because of budgetary needs or you were called up to do surveillance on short notice before you could arrange for additional personnel. This kind of situation certainly makes your job harder, but let me give you a little idea that I fell into last year in San Francisco.

After teaching a seminar session for the account executives of Prentice Hall On-line in San Francisco, we all went to dinner at a "killer" restaurant that had the best pasta that ever hit my mouth. Of course, we washed this down with a goodly amount of wine and came back to our hotel with more than just a little bit of a buzz on. I successfully negotiated the lobby, rode up on the elevator to the eleventh floor, and then drew a total blank. I knew that this was my floor, but I had no idea of my room number. I fished my plastic card key out of my pocket (all hotels are now going to these access cards because they can be reprogrammed daily, for each new customer, without having to rekey the hotel rooms), and saw that there was no room number on the key.

Feeling slightly stupid, I picked up the house phone and called the operator to ask what room I was in. My voice was a little slurred, it was almost midnight, and I explained to the night operator that I didn't want to fumble around the floor, trying my key in five other people's rooms before getting lucky or getting punched out by some big dude who thought I was trying to burglarize his room. Amazingly, the sweet voice on the other end of the phone told me I was in Room 1158 as she laughed at my little situation.

As soon as I snapped to what she'd done, I sobered up in a heartbeat with a realization that I had just figured out a new way to find out a target's hotel rooms. Since that time, I've tried this little game in every hotel from Seattle to St. Louis and found that it works almost every time. Just sound a little sheepish, slightly tipsy, and do it late at night when people would expect you to be drunk and it works almost every time.

When it comes to equipment, I bow to my good friend Bill Kizorek of In-Photo. Bill's company has photographed more injury claims than any firm I know and has invested more than $4 million in cameras and surveillance equipment of all kinds. Through trial and error, Kizorek's staff has gone from VHS to 8mm, both for its size and its ease of operation. But Kizorek warns, "Video equipment changes every few years. After we bought 50 Sony EVCX-7 8mm cameras, no more were made with 'c' mount lenses."

For those of you who have VHS equipment or like the convenience of popping the tape right in your home video recorder, there is some fairly new equipment that stands head and shoulders above the 8x to 12x equipment that most of us see in the store. A growing number of manufacturers today are selling 64x digital VHS recorders, equipment that provides the investigator with a dynamite field of view and the telephoto ability to read a newspaper from almost a block away.

While going through one of my discount catalogs last week, I saw a Hitachi 64x video recorder for $895, about one-third of what most of us paid for surveillance cameras only a few years ago. Before buying camera equipment, it pays to do a little research. Check out *Consumer Reports* and other consumer guides, as well as reputable camera stores in your area.

For those of you who want to learn more about the personal injury investigative business, I recommend several books written by Bill Kizorek that explain, in far greater detail, the psychology and makeup of the personal injury claimant. Bill has been documenting injury claims for almost 20 years and is undoubtedly one of the true experts in this field. Additionally, he is a great guy, has helped many investigators learn this business throughout the country by speaking at investigative seminars, and has shared his knowledge by writing these investigative bibles. (See Bibliography for the titles of Kizorek's books.)

Incidently, Bill says the most important key to successful surveillance is "to stay out of sight. Sitting in the front seat of a car draws a lot of attention to you. Vans are much better." A free piece of advice from the master.

CHAPTER 16

Insurance Investigation

he ultimate goal of any insurance investigation is to determine the facts and circumstances pertinent to a claim and document the validity (or inaccuracy) of a claimant's case. To perform this job properly, the investigator should examine the circumstances leading up to the filing of the claim, the details of the claim itself, and the extent of damage or disability that continues after the incident on which the claimant's case is based once he is stabilized.

The term "insurance" is defined by *Webster's Dictionary* as:

1. Insuring or being insured
2. A contract (insurance policy) whereby compensation is guaranteed to the insured for a specified loss by fire, death, etc.
3. The amount for which something is insured
4. The premium paid for an insurance policy
5. The business of insurance against loss

The initial phase of the investigation, the examination of the circumstances leading up to the filing of a claim, determines the extent of any pre-existing conditions that would have a bearing on the validity of the issuance of the insurance policy. Any conditions that, revealed to the insurance company, would have caused the insurers to have denied the issuance of the policy or rated it as a higher risk are pertinent to this type of investigation.

A good example of these circumstances is often found in life and health investigations concerning death claims. In one particular case, the insured claimed to be a nonsmoker, thereby enjoying a substantially lower life insurance rate, but later died of lung cancer. Examination of the background of the policyholder and interview of the people who had personal knowledge of the claimant found him to be a heavy smoker.

This information was also confirmed by the autopsy report of the medical examiner's office and led to the denial of the claim.

The examination of the incident leading up to the claim will focus on the specifics of the activities of the claimant on or about the time of the claim. This is done to determine if the insured's actions were contributory to the claim or could the incident or accident have been avoided under normal circumstances. Investigators are also interested in determining if the incident was truly an accident or did the insured create the circumstances and cause the accident to happen as a setup claim.

What are some of the indicators of fraudulent claims or cases that require further investigation? This checklist outlines many of the "red flags" found by insurance investigators to be indicative of potential fraud. When a combination of three or more of these indicators exist, it's time for further investigation, which means money in your pocket.

If you really want to be smart, share with your clients this list of red flags that every employer should be aware of and use it as a basis of examining employee injuries.

1. Receipt of Accident Board Application
2. Physical Evidence
3. Conflicting Versions
4. Injury Occurs and There Is No Witness
5. Refuses Company Doctor
6. Refuses Settlement Offer
7. Never at Home

Another scale that insurers and employers should consider in examining their claims is the type of circumstances that most often lead to employee claims. Frequently, a set of circumstances will trigger a rash of claims as follows:

1. Employee Terminated
2. Disability
3. Near Retirement
4. Short Term of Employment
5. Many Prior Similar Claims

Workman's Compensation Can Work for You

ne of the greatest problems our clients face is the rise in workman's compensation rates and the tremendous increase in employee claims and litigation seen in the past two years.

In reviewing new legislation and speaking with other investigators throughout the state, I feel that this legislation is a good start but is not going to be a cure for all employers. It is just the start of a program that we can assist our clients to develop if they are going to survive in business. With this program, we must also institute an internal program to identify suspicious claims and establish a means to examine the legitimacy or fraudulent nature of these injuries.

Through years of investigating such claims, both as an employer and as a professional investigator (yes, we have had claims, too), I have developed a list of red flags that every employer should be aware of and use as a basis of examining employee injuries. A number of these red flags are the same as for insurance fraud claims discussed in the previous chapter:

1. Receipt of accident board application was first notice of injury—employee did not notify the employer of the injury through normal channels or on the day of the job injury itself.
2. Physical evidence conflicts with presented facts—employee claims injuries that are not found or diagnosed by the physician examining the employee for specific claims.
3. Conflicting versions of the incident by witnesses—other employees' observation of the claimant or the accident differs dramatically from the injury claimed by the employee.
4. An injury occurs and there are no witnesses—employee claims to have been working alone and there is no physical evidence of

injury or damage observable to the employee or company equipment.

5. Refuses to go to company doctor or obtain second medical opinion—employee goes to his own doctor, refuses to see company physician or accept rehabilitation recommended by the physician.

6. Refuses to accept an offer to return to work in another capacity, temporarily or permanently—employee refuses to discuss other employment and will not negotiate with employer for other acceptable positions.

7. Claimant is never at home to receive phone calls after injury—employer attempts to contact claimant at home to determine his work potential or medical rehabilitation program but can never find employee at home when he calls.

When you as an employer see several of the above red flags, it's time to examine the claimant more closely to determine if he is truly injured, is taking a vacation on your company payroll, or has started new employment in a job not reported to you or the employment commission.

Another scale that the prudent employer should consider in examining his claims is the type of circumstances that most often lead to employee claims. Frequently, a set of circumstances will trigger a rash of claims as follows:

1. Employee was terminated before first notice of injury. The injury claim comes in after the employee has been released from his job. Some employees use this excuse to milk months of employment benefits from an employer that has terminated them for cause.

2. Disability occurred just prior to a period of layoffs or discontinuation of seasonal work. Employee's knowing that the company is going to be laying off employees frequently file claims, prior to this period of layoffs so that they can again extract months of benefits after employment is over.

3. Employee is near retirement. What better way for an employee to draw a double retirement than to have an injury as well as his company retirement plan?

4. Short term of employment prior to injury or prior listing of self employment. Many professional plaintiffs join a work force just to get on the benefits program and consider workman's compensation and disability a major benefit and source of income. (Do you want to hire one of these people?)

5. Employees with many prior similar claims with previous employers. Employees with a history of claims with the IAB or in civil suits don't often change their spots with the new employer; they only get better as time goes on.

What are some of the things that you can do as an investigator to help your employer to avoid all this mess? How can you keep your injury rate within bounds and insurance ratios within acceptable means? Let me suggest several ideas that you can use to protect your clients from these series of claims.

1. Institute an employee-screening program to identify applicants with a previous history of claims with the IAB or similar criminal suits in their previous areas of residence or employment.

2. Institute a preventative safety training program and reward employees or work areas that consistently have a low number of claims.

3. Provide information relating to safety prevention tools, aides, and equipment at each work sight and enforce safety rules through supervisory personnel.

4. Require employee notification of accident, injury, or safety violations on company facilities. Require supervisory personnel to conduct on-site examination to determine the nature, extent, and cause of injury and to document witnesses and circumstances of injury at the time of incident.

5. Designate an employee safety officer to review all incidents, accidents, or safety

claims and to prepare a weekly summary of such claims to company executives, as well as recommendations to prevent future accidents.

6. Examine and investigate suspicious claims to document employee status, accident circumstances, and claimant current status.

If you will develop and implement a program that follows these guidelines, you will see a reduction of up to 50 percent in both the frequency and longevity of your client's employee claims. The implementation of these programs, the majority of which can be conducted through existing personnel with no loss to their workload, is the single most cost-effective method of controlling your clients worker's compensation cost and your own injury claims in your company.

Interview or Interrogate

hat is the difference between an interview and an interrogation? Most of us see an interview as something that is done in a pleasant surrounding, by people with smiling faces who are sharing information in a nonconfrontational manner. When we hear the term interrogation, we think of bright lights, rubber hoses, and the SS officer in the black leather trench coat uttering that famous line, "Ve have vays of making you talk."

The rule of thumb that many investigators go by is that an interview is something you do to third parties having knowledge of a subject, and an interrogation is reserved for the subject of that investigation. The interviews are used to gather information about the subject and to ask those probing questions that make the interrogation successful if the subject is showing signs of deception.

One of the key elements in conducting an internal investigation, or any investigation in which you are trying to determine if one of a number of people are doing something wrong, is to develop the information already in the minds of their co-workers, the people they work with everyday.

The people having the most direct and detailed knowledge of the daily activities of anyone are the employees and personal friends that see your subject on a regular basis. Our job is then to determine the opinions and knowledge of these employees by asking a series of questions designed to get their suspicions, intuition, and gut feelings in a nonintrusive, noncombative form through a series of questions that tell us what they know, without them knowing why we want it.

To overcome the reluctance on the part of many people to talk about their suspicions about other people or to specifically name an individual that they believe is involved in wrongdoing, we have developed an

		1	2	3	4	5	6	7	8	9	10
1	Tom Smith	X	8	8	7	9	4	7	6	9	8
2	Bob Jones	9	X	7	5	8	5	8	5	8	9
3	Al Long	8	9	X	8	9	6	8	6	9	8
4	Cindy Roe	5	7	6	X	6	9	6	8	6	6
5	Joe Todd	8	8	8	7	X	5	8	9	9	8
6	Bill West	5	6	6	9	7	X	5	6	4	5
7	Lisa Stuart	8	9	8	6	7	4	X	9	8	8
8	Jennie Best	8	7	7	6	9	5	8	X	9	9
9	Ed Short	9	8	9	6	9	6	8	9	X	8
10	Tom Harper	8	9	8	7	9	4	9	9	8	X

EJP/cjp.039

interviewing technique that identifies those parties that fall outside the parameters of accepted peer behavior and thus helps identify those people that the interviewed party believes may be involved in or is responsible for the problems we are investigating.

The key to this interviewing technique, which I call the "queen for a day," is a peer-rating system in which the interviewed party appoints a numerical value to each person whom they work with or have knowledge of in their daily activities. These interviewed parties then rate those individuals on a point scale of one to ten based on their general, overall, nonspecific perceptions, impressions, and gut feelings that tell us whom they suspect of being the cause of our client's problems.

This queen-for-a-day interviewing and rating system identifies individuals whom other people rate outside the norm or standard awarded to the majority of other people they know or work with, and it allows the investigator to determine whom the majority of employees or other people rate most poorly. Through this interview technique and its rating system, people identify the individuals they feel are responsible for problems that they perceive.

This queen-for-a-day technique is so named because the interviewer tells the employee or knowledgeable party that, for the purposes of this interview, the interviewed party has just been promoted to the position of supervisor, manager, or president of the company. The "queen" is to rate every other person in the company based on the personal perceptions and impressions of each employee. The interviewed party assigns a one as a lowest rating and a ten as the highest rating of the other parties based on their impressions and preferences.

This interviewing technique is a useful tool that helps to focus the initial investigation on parties that the majority of other people believe fall outside the accepted behavior pattern, so that investigators can then concentrate their investigation on those that the majority suspect. If the majority of the co-workers rate an individual lowest in the group, then this tells the investigator that the majority feel that some activity has or may have taken place, that they disapprove of this individual in some way, or that they have knowledge that this person is really a dirtbag.

After interviewing all of the employees or potential parties, the investigator determines the party or parties who scored the lowest on this peer rating system and then examines the ratings assigned by those low-scoring parties in comparison to the others in the test program. If these lowest-rated individuals rate other employees in a range contrary to the majority, the investigator now knows those parties that the lowest-rated individual (and highest potential suspect) feels closest to and most comfortable with. These individuals are often found to be closely related to the activities or dealings of this prime suspect. These findings also indicate that the person scored most highly by the lowest-rated person and also rated lowly by other peers are those often involved as an assistant or co-conspirator with the lowest-rated suspect.

EDMUND J. PANKAU, CFE –
INTERTECT, INC.
5300 MEMORIAL DR #450
HOUSTON, TX. 77007
713-880-1111

	1	2	3	4	5	6	7	8	9	10
1										
2										
3										
4										
5										
6										
7										
8										
9										
10										

Once the abnormal or lowest-rated persons are identified through this interviewing technique, then further interviews of a more in-depth and probing nature can be used to determine the nature and extent of the concerns or problems known by the interviewed parties and to determine which employees have the most knowledge of problem areas or would be most cooperative in helping in the investigations of the subjects. This technique is very simple to use and master.

Once understood and practiced, this can be an extremely effective tool for any investigator, auditor, or fraud examiner and is an excellent training tool for developing higher levels of investigative interviewing techniques.

The chart on page 90 shows a series of interviews of 10 employees and the ratings assigned by each of them to each other.

From this chart, we can quickly see that number six (Bill West) was rated lowest by his peers. West in turn highly rated number four

(Cindy Row), who was also rated low by other workers. By concentrating our investigation on West, we found that he was indeed the person responsible for the theft of company seismic data and that Cindy had helped copy and attempted to sell the information to another company.

The rules of this test are as follows:

1. Score people only by number 1-10, with 1 being superbad and 10 being supergood. Base it on gut feelings, intuition, hunches, or something you can't explain.

2. Explain, if asked, that you are evaluating negatives such as lies, exaggerations, bragging, thefts, insincerity, and just being sneaky.

3. All numbers are kept confidential.

4. Start with yourself first, and just do numbers only, no reasons this time.

I have used this technique for more than 12 years and have shared it with hundreds of other investigators around the country. One of them recently used this simple technique in the investigation of drug losses from a hospital pharmacy and, in her first tests, identified the ultimate person found to be responsible for the thefts.

If you don't believe me, just try it sometime. You will find that this is the single best interviewing technique for fishing for information and will point to the problem people and problem areas almost every time.

Filling in the Gaps

f things get a little slow for you at one time or another, or you need to find some extra work for the new investigator you've just hired, there are a number of ancillary areas of investigation that help to bring in the bacon and pay the bills.

Several of these areas, if pursued diligently, will result in a whole new area of business and a full-time job if you want it.

PROCESS SERVING

The most common fill-in work, found with every law firm in the United States, is serving court papers, namely witness subpoenas, citations, petitions, and complaints. Every attorney has experienced the nightmare of dealing with the local sheriff or constable who only serves papers Monday through Friday, during normal business hours. Deputies don't make any extra money for additional effort (unless you give it to them), so most of them don't stalk their subject or take the extra effort to make sure the papers are served in a timely manner or on a rush basis when you need it desperately.

You can easily charge $25 to $50 per paper in most parts of the country for serving witness subpoenas and federal citations (state papers, too, if your law allows) for attorneys and court reporters and often pick up extra money for locating a good address on the parties because the address the attorney had was three years old.

Every Friday, right at closing time, I get at least one call from a local attorney to serve a dozen subpoenas over the weekend for trial Monday morning. You see, lawyers are lazy and always wait to the last minute before getting ready for trial.

In a lot of cases, new clients don't have a good address (it's three years old, given to them by their clients when they filed the suit), and haven't had any contact with the witnesses for months. This is where your investigative library comes in. By having those voter registration and utility microfiche, you can quickly locate most of the witnesses and ask them if they know the other witnesses' current address when you serve them. Now you can charge your client a double fee for both locating and serving his papers, and it gives you a great opportunity to hit on him to use you for all of his investigative work in the future.

If you're real smart, you'll strike up a relationship with one of the local court reporters who prepares the witness subpoenas and deposition subpoenas for your local lawyers and make a deal with them to serve all of their papers for a reduced fee. Many of the court reporting firms will have 10 to 50 court reporters working for them and service anywhere from 50 to 100 or more attorneys. A good court-reporting firm can bring you enough business to fill up all of your spare time and possibly provide full-time jobs for several young investigators you'd like to hire but just don't have the work for.

A word of advice: pay your process servers by the paper served. If your lawyer pays you $40, split it with the process server—half for you for bringing in the business and half for him for serving the paper. If you charge mileage, give it all to the process server because it costs that much or more to run his car everyday.

Unless you can charge your client for all of the billable hours incurred in process serving, it's not profitable to pay hourly rates for process service.

COLLECTING ON COURT JUDGMENTS

Another potential source of income for investigators comes by way of checking the judgment records of debtors in the county courthouse. In the real property records at the county recorder's office, you will find page after page of recorded judgments that are probably uncollected at this time.

Since you are down at the courthouse anyway, at least once in awhile, it pays to check the names of people who are judgment debtors against the data bases that may disclose their assets.

By searching four data bases (corporate officers and directors, assumed name filings, tax assessor, and probate), you can quickly determine any new business names or tangible assets in the name of the debtor and make a nice fee by matching the assets to the creditor of the judgment.

Once you determine that a debtor has possible assets, it's a simple matter to call either the owner of the judgment or the attorney who obtained it and make an offer. He won't often refuse. For 25 to 50 percent of the judgment, based on the dollar value, you will provide documentation of the assets. All you have to do is draw up a simple contract by which both parties agree that you will collect your fee against any assets that are recovered as a result of the information you provide to the client.

If you are wondering if this is a pipe dream or a real way of making money, I know several investigators who make a comfortable living doing nothing but this kind of business in their spare time. My own experience, with an asphalt-paving contractor who gave me 100 judgments, was that more than half of the debtors either remarried, started a new business, or inherited assets from their parents in a two-year period during which I tracked these cases. My fees came close to $50,000 after all was said and done. Not bad for an hour's work once a week, spot-checking these people a few at a time, until they came into some money.

One thing I learned from this is that almost all con men never stay broke. They go up and down the financial scale, being a high roller when they've got money or living off someone else when they are broke. The trick is to catch them when they've just scored on a big deal and come into something of value. That's why you've got to check them in the court records or drive by their houses to see if there is any change in their life-style and then jump right on them when you find something. Their new-found wealth might be gone tomorrow!

WHAT NOT TO DO

Several years ago, a well-known divorce lawyer called me late at night and asked if I could be in his office first thing the next morning. He had just been woken up by his client, who said that he was being blackmailed and wanted somebody to figure out what was happening right away.

At 8:00 the next morning, bright and shiny, I was in the lawyer's office and listened to the client tell me how he had received a telephone call from a person purporting to be a private investigator who wanted to sell him some information about his wife. It seems that this "private investigator" just happened to be conducting a little surveillance on the local grocery store parking lot and saw our client's wife wheel into the lot. Several minutes later, another car pulled up along side hers, and she got out of her car and into the embrace of the driver of the second car.

Our "investigator" just happened to write down both of the license plate numbers and ran them the next morning. For curiosity's sake, he searched the records to see if they were married, found their home addresses and phone numbers, and was now offering his services to the client with whom I was meeting.

"What's going on?" asked the client. "Is this guy for real? Why was he in the lot looking at my wife, and do you think this is really true?"

Having seen this several times before, I informed our clients that this is one of the ways that some not-so-ethical investigators pick up extra money. You see, you can go to almost any shopping center parking lot in the country and wait until it gets dark to see the fun begin. Almost every night, you can see two cars pull in, and their drivers sneak a quick kiss and take off in one of the cars to have, in the words of a famous rock song, "a third-rate romance, low-rent rendezvous."

My client was torn between a choice of breaking the investigator's legs or paying him $500 to find out who his wife was fooling around with. Every time he thought about this deal, it made him madder, and before long, he was going to punch somebody out. The only question was, would it be his wife or the caller?

We settled the matter by having me call the phone number, which was answered by an answering service employee who only knew to call a pager number, whose owner would get back to me. I explained to our anonymous caller that he was about to get in deep kimchee and that his little sideline income was about to cause him some hospitalization. I suggested to Mr. Anonymous that he forget trying to put the squeeze on my client, his wife, or the other party she met as well. We had a brief discussion about ethics and the law, and I convinced him that I could figure out who he really was with just a little work and that he really didn't want to have me do this. He soon realized that it would be in his best interest to find a new sideline.

It must have worked, because I never heard from our friend again. It's a good thing, too. Little did our anonymous little investigator know that the pigeon he was trying to squeeze in this case was a former defensive linebacker in the pros. Had this man hit this guy, like he had so many quarterbacks in years past, our friend would not have been a happy camper.

Managing Your Best Assets— Your People

The reason most investigators never grow beyond the level of a one-man (or woman) mom and pop business is that they don't have employees to back them up and enhance their own efforts. These investigators don't realize that good employees are their greatest asset and the key to growth.

Everyday I hear some investigator bitching about someone whom he trained for three years leaving him and taking two or three of his clients. Just when this assistant was really becoming good at the business, POOF, off he went.

"Well," I ask the one complaining, "what did you expect? You paid him as contract labor, only for hours billed, made him report his own taxes, and gave him no benefits after he busted his butt night after night on graveyard surveillance cases. He watched you take all the glory and the money, and you expect him to stay? Forget it!"

EMPLOYEE BENEFITS

If you want to grow beyond the reach of your own two hands, think of the people who work for you as assets, not liabilities. Ask them what they want out of the business, a raise or an insurance plan that covers major medical, dental, and prescription drugs. When I asked this of my staff, they wanted the benefits, and I found that it was much cheaper for me, as an employer, to get them than for my employees on their own.

I appointed one of my investigators, a former insurance adjuster, to get several bids and ideas on insurance plans, and he came up with a great idea that we use to this day. He found an employee-leasing company called Administaff that could manage our payroll, fill out all our

have salaried employees or benefit plans.)

SHARING THE WEALTH

Beyond your benefit program,
share the wealth once in a while.
When one of those big cases
scores, share the praise and profits
with the people who made it happen. Let your good investigators
do the case in Cancun once in a
while, or share the wealth when a

THE MOST VALUABLE ASSET OF ANY COM-
PANY IS NOT THE INVENTORY OR CAPITAL
OR BUILDING OR EVEN THE CLIENT LIST. IT
IS THE EMPLOYEES WHO WORK THERE.

tax forms, and provide a dynamite comprehensive insurance
plan, cheaper than we could get
insurance alone. This program
let us eliminate one employee
position (payroll/bookkeeping),
cut our worker's compensation
rate by 30 percent (by pooling us
with other companies), and provided us with a major medical
plan that is now my edge in getting and keeping other investigators and employees. (You
see, none of the other PI firms around here

client pays in gold coins (one for you, one for
you, one for you, three for me) or some other
coin of the realm.

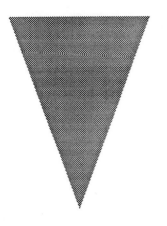

Summary

hrough using the techniques and procedures that I've outlined in this book, I've watched my investigative agency grow from a "one-man band" into one of the most successful agencies of its kind in the business.

When I started this company, I had no idea that someday I would manage a business with more employees than I had fingers and toes and a payroll that exceeded a million dollars a year.

What I have learned through trial and error and a great deal of luck and perseverance is now offered to you with the hope that you add to our knowledge something of your own and share it with your associates and friends.

If I've missed something that you either want to know more about or can add to, you can usually find me in my Houston office, as long as I'm not out on an investigation or speaking tour.

My address is as follows:

Edmund J. Pankau
Intertect, Inc.
5300 Memorial Dr., Suite 450
Houston, Texas 77007

Forms and Contracts

Readers' response to the first edition of this book was terrific. But many readers did ask me to include samples of forms and contracts that we use at Intertect for various investigative techniques. So I have selected those forms that we use most often and that I believe will be of most benefit to investigators.

To use these forms, just replace the name of my firm, Intertect, with that of yours and make any additions, deletions, or modifications that will help you to do your job better.

INTERTECT, INC. - REQUEST FOR SERVICES AGREEMENT

SENDER: CONTRACTOR _____

INTERTECT, INC.   _____
5300 MEMORIAL DR. #450
HOUSTON, TX 77007   _____
713-880-1111
FAX 713-880-2805   _____

SERVICE: _____ Surveillance _____ Account Search _____ Data Base Srch
_____ Public Records Search _____ Locate _____ General Investigation

_____ State Corp Filings   _____ State UCC Filings   _____ Interview
_____ Officer/Dir Filings   _____ County UCC Filings   _____ Take statmt
_____ County D/B/A's   _____ Criminal History   _____ Civil Litgn
_____ Tax Assessor   _____ Felony/Misdemeanor   County/State/Fed
_____ Probate   _____ Real Property Srch   _____ Lien/Jdgmt
_____ Prof. Licenses   _____ Medical History   _____ Bankruptcy
_____ Our Forms Attached*

CONDUCT WORK IN: _____

OTHER: _____

* USE OUR FORMS - DO NOT FURNISH A WRITTEN REPORT

AUTHORIZED BILLING INFORMATION: Fixed Fee Rate : $ _____ Hourly: $ _____

Max: $ _____ Tax: _____% Cost Per Mile: $ _____

Case #: _____   SUBJECT OF INVESTIGATION

Date of Request:_____   NAME _____

Due Date:_____   ADDRESS _____

                                  CITY/ST/ZIP _____
RETURN INFO AND INVOICE TO:
                                  SSN/DOB _____
    Intertect, Inc.
    P.O. BOX 131016   OTHER _____
    HOUSTON, TX. 77007
    PHONE 713-880-1111   _____
    FAX 713-880-2805
                                  _____
ATTN:
VIA: Telephone/FAX/Express Mail   _____
Regular Mail

PLEASE READ THE FOLLOWING SECTION CAREFULLY:

All requests for services, service fees and instructions for services
to be rendered by the contractor will constitute this agreement. Your
signature below indicates your acceptance to the terms and conditions
of this agreement. Invoices rendered for work performed, will be paid
45 days from the invoice date. Please insure your invoice contains your
Tax ID# or SSN. A copy of this agreement must accompany your invoice.
Invoices billed over the authorized amount will be returned for correct-
ion. Our firm does not recognize interest charges on invoices unless a
contract for same is executed in advance. Please bill all other expenses
other than those above, at cost. Receipts may be requested for payment.
Please annotate in the block above the state tax rate for this service,
if applicable. The fixed fee rate above is maximum, please include all
expenses and taxes within that figure. If fixed fee research, you must
use our provided research forms and do not execute a written report.
Late results, forms not utilized, or incorrect invoicing, may delay payment. If charges are expected to exceed this authorization, contact the
sender prior to expenditure.

_____   _____
    (Date)   Contractor's Acceptance Signature

INTERTECT, INC.
HOURLY SERVICE AGREEMENT

Agreement is made this date _____, 1992 between

Intertect, Inc. and _____ of the

firm of _____,
herein after referred to as "client", to conduct the following
services in the following jurisdictions:

_____

_____

_____

_____

The following are billing rates for those services plus a 8.25%
sales tax if the work is conducted in Texas:

    Management Investigative: Billable at $ _____ per hour
    Senior Investigative: Billable at $ _____ per hour
    Staff/Researcher: Billable at $ _____ per hour
    Administrative: Billable at $ _____ per hour

                                Maximum Budget $ _____

Expenses are defined as:
    Mileage: Billable at $ _____ per mile
    Copies: Billable at $ _____ per copy

Other expenses, such as long distance telephone charges, FAX,
data base search fees, etc., are billable at cost incurred by
Intertect, Inc.

The above fees will be incurred and payable by the client regardless
of the outcome of the service. Intertect, Inc. will not warranty the
information concerned in the records of the particular jurisdiction
in which the client has requested the service take place.

This agreement is made between Intertect, Inc., and the client.
Fees and expenses billed/invoiced to the client are the responsibility of same and are due and payable by the client within thirty
days of the date of the invoice. Invoices remaining unpaid after
thirty days may incur a 1.5% interest charge per month on the unpaid balance.

_____   _____
Client Name   Intertect, Inc.   Name

Intertect, Inc. is licensed by the Texas Board of Private
Investigators and Private Security Agencies, P.O. Box 13509
Capitol Station, Austin, Texas 78711 (512) 463-5545

INVESTIGATORS REPORT

CASE # _____ SUBJECT _____

DATE IN __/__/__ DATE OUT __/__/__ INVESTIGATOR _____

PERSONAL HISTORY
        FULL NAME _____

ADDRESS _____

DOB _____ SS# _____ SPOUSE _____
                                            Voter reg / marriage

BUSINESS HISTORY

CORPORATIONS _____

_____

UCC _____

_____

LITIGATION HISTORY

CIVIL - SMALL CLAIMS _____

      SUPERIOR _____

      FEDERAL _____

      BANKRUPTCY _____

LIENS / JUDGMENTS _____

CRIMINAL (if requested)

TAX ASSESSOR _____

REAL PROPERTY _____

_____

PROBATE _____

BANKING _____

INVESTIGATIVE DISCOVERY

INTERTECT, INC. - 5300 MEMORIAL DR. #450, HOUSTON, TX. 77007
Phone 713/880-1111   Fax 713/880-2805

INTERTECT, INC. - LOCATE FORM

CASE # _____ AGENT _____ DATE _____

SUBJECT _____

ADDRESS _____ CITY _____ ST/ZIP _____

DOB _____ SS# _____ SPOUSE _____

TELEPHONE BOOK	
CRISS CROSS DIR.	
VOTER REG.	
ASSUMED/CORP NAMES	
ELECTRIC/UTILITY	
WATER/GAS UTILITY	
DRIVERS LICENSE	
CREDIT /SS TRACE	
EMPLOYMENT/LICENSING BOARDS	
STATE EMPLOYMENT COMMISSION	
NOTARY REGISTRATION	
POST OFFICE (FOIA REQUEST)	
MARRIAGE/DIVORCE RECORDS	
CIVIL SUITS & ATTY	
CRIMINAL RECORDS & BONDSMAN	
UCC'S & BANK	
REAL PROPERTY	
NEWSPAPER INDEXES	

*** ATTACH COPIES OR WRITTEN INFORMATION TO THIS REPORT ***

EX SPOUSE _____ FORMER EMPLOYER _____

FAMILY MEMBERS _____ FORMER CO-WORKER _____

FAMILY MEMBER _____ FORMER BANKS _____

NEIGHBORS _____

MISCELLANEOUS RECORDS RESEARCH FORM   CASE # _____   INV _____

SUBJECT _____   SPOUSE _____

VOTER REGISTRATION

NAME: _____

_____

ADDRESS: _____

_____

CITY/ZIP _____

DOB: _____

SS# _____

PHONE # _____

_____

MARRIAGE LICENSE

HUSBAND NAME _____

ADDRESS_____

_____

_____

CITY/ZIP _____

PROOF OF ID:_____

DOB _____

SS# _____

PHONE # _____

TELEPHONE DIRECTORY

NAME: _____

_____

ADDRESS _____

_____

PHONE #: _____

COMMENTS: _____

_____

WIFE NAME _____

ADDRESS_____

_____

_____

PROOF OF ID_____

DOB _____

SS#_____

PUBLIC UTILITIES

NAME: _____

_____

ADDRESS: _____

_____

CITY/ZIP _____

SS# _____

PHONE # _____

COMMENTS _____

_____

PUBLIC UTILITIES

NAME: _____

_____

ADDRESS: _____

_____

CITY/ZIP _____

SS# _____

PHONE # _____

COMMENTS _____

_____

SECRETARY OF STATE - SUBJECT _____ CASE # _____ INV ___

CORP NAME _____

_____

_____

_____

CHARTER # _____

STATUS _____

DATE OF FILING _____

ADDRESS _____

_____

CITY/ZIP _____

_____

PARENT/SUBSIDIARY_____

_____

OFFICERS_____

_____

_____

_____

COMMENTS _____

_____

_____

_____

_____

_____

CORP NAME _____

_____

_____

_____

CHARTER # _____

STATUS _____

DATE OF FILING _____

ADDRESS _____

_____

CITY/ZIP _____

_____

PARENT/SUBSIDIARY _____

_____

OFFICERS _____

_____

_____

_____

COMMENTS _____

_____

_____

_____

_____

_____

ASSUMED NAME - SUBJECT _____ CASE # _____ INV _____

FILE #. _____

COMPANY NAME _____

_____

_____

ADDRESS_____

_____

_____

TYPE BUSINESS_____

OWNERS _____

_____

_____

DATE FILED _____

ABANDON DATE _____

FILE # _____

COMPANY NAME _____

_____

_____

ADDRESS_____

_____

_____

TYPE BUSINESS_____

OWNERS _____

_____

_____

DATE FILED _____

ABANDON DATE _____

FILE # _____

COMPANY NAME _____

_____

_____

ADDRESS_____

_____

_____

TYPE BUSINESS_____

OWNERS _____

_____

_____

DATE FILED _____

ABANDON DATE _____

FILE # _____

COMPANY NAME _____

_____

_____

ADDRESS_____

_____

_____

TYPE BUSINESS_____

OWNERS _____

_____

_____

DATE FILED _____

ABANDON DATE _____

UCC RESEARCH FORM

SUBJECT _____ CASE # _____ INV _____

STATE COUNTY
INSTRUMENT # _____

DEBTOR _____

_____

SECURED PARTY _____

_____

DATE FILED _____

SECURED INTEREST _____

_____

_____

_____

EXPER DATE _____

STATE COUNTY
INSTRUMENT # _____

DEBTOR _____

_____

SECURED PARTY _____

_____

DATE FILED _____

SECURED INTEREST _____

_____

_____

_____

EXPER DATE _____

STATE COUNTY
INSTRUMENT # _____

DEBTOR _____

_____

SECURED PARTY _____

_____

DATE FILED _____

SECURED INTEREST _____

_____

_____

_____

EXPER DATE _____

STATE COUNTY
INSTRUMENT # _____

DEBTOR _____

_____

SECURED PARTY _____

_____

DATE FILED _____

SECURED INTEREST _____

_____

_____

_____

EXPER DATE _____

LITIGATION - SUBJECT _____ CASE # _____ INV ____

| CTY   DIST   FED   PROBATE | CTY DIST   FED   PROBATE |
| CIVIL   CRIMINAL | CIVIL   CRIMINAL |

CAUSE # _____

STYLE _____

_____

_____

DATE FILED _____

COURT # _____

TYPE CASE _____

_____

PLAINTIFF LAWYER _____

_____

TELEPHONE_____

_____

DEFENDANT LAWYER _____

_____

TELEPHONE_____

_____

JUDGMENTS _____

_____

STATUS _____

SUMMARY _____

_____

_____

_____

_____

_____

CAUSE # _____

STYLE _____

_____

_____

DATE FILED _____

COURT # _____

TYPE CASE _____

_____

PLAINTIFF LAWYER _____

_____

TELEPHONE_____

_____

DEFENDANT LAWYER _____

_____

TELEPHONE_____

_____

JUDGMENTS _____

_____

STATUS _____

SUMMARY _____

_____

_____

_____

_____

_____

JUDGMENT RESEARCH FORM

SUBJECT _____   CASE # _____ INV _____

JUDGMENTS: CTY   DIST   FED

CAUSE # _____

PLAINTIFF _____

_____

_____

DEFENDANT _____

_____

_____

DATE FILED _____

TYPE SUIT _____

_____

JUDGMENTS _____

_____

JUDGMENTS: CTY   DIST   FED

CAUSE # _____

PLAINTIFF _____

_____

_____

DEFENDANT _____

_____

_____

DATE FILED _____

TYPE SUIT _____

_____

JUDGMENTS _____

_____

JUDGMENTS: CTY   DIST   FED

CAUSE # _____

PLAINTIFF _____

_____

_____

DEFENDANT _____

_____

_____

DATE FILED _____

TYPE SUIT _____

_____

JUDGMENTS _____

_____

JUDGMENTS: CTY   DIST   FED

CAUSE # _____

PLAINTIFF _____

_____

_____

DEFENDANT _____

_____

_____

DATE FILED _____

TYPE SUIT _____

_____

JUDGMENTS _____

_____

ATTACHMENT _____   FT/JDGLN   REV 1-6-90

TAX ASSESSOR - SUBJECT _____ CASE # _____ INV _____

OWNER _____

_____

LEGAL _____

_____

_____

ADDRESS _____

_____

CITY/ST/ZIP _____

VALUATION _____

TAX YEAR ___19_____

HOMESTEAD   YES _____   NO _____

COMMENTS _____

_____

OWNER _____

_____

LEGAL _____

_____

_____

ADDRESS _____

_____

CITY/ST/ZIP _____

VALUATION _____

TAX YEAR ___19_____

HOMESTEAD   YES _____   NO _____

COMMENTS _____

_____

OWNER _____

_____

LEGAL _____

_____

_____

ADDRESS _____

_____

CITY/ST/ZIP _____

VALUATION _____

TAX YEAR ___19_____

HOMESTEAD   YES _____   NO _____

COMMENTS _____

_____

OWNER _____

_____

LEGAL _____

_____

_____

ADDRESS _____

_____

CITY/ST/ZIP _____

VALUATION _____

TAX YEAR ___19_____

HOMESTEAD   YES _____   NO _____

COMMENTS _____

_____

REAL PROPERTY - SUBJECT _____ CASE # _____ INV _____

RECORD # _____

LEGAL DESCRIP _____

_____

DOCUMENT _____

GRANTOR _____

_____

GRANTEE _____

_____

DATE FILED _____

STREET ADD _____

AMT/MTG _____

COMMENTS _____

_____

RECORD # _____

LEGAL DESCRIP _____

_____

DOCUMENT: _____

GRANTOR _____

_____

GRANTEE _____

_____

DATE FILED _____

STREET ADD _____

AMT/MTG _____

COMMENTS _____

_____

RECORD # _____

LEGAL DESCRIP _____

_____

DOCUMENT _____

GRANTOR _____

_____

GRANTEE _____

_____

DATE FILED _____

STREET ADD _____

AMT/MTG _____

COMMENTS _____

_____

RECORD # _____

LEGAL DESCRIP _____

_____

DOCUMENT _____

GRANTOR _____

_____

GRANTEE _____

_____

DATE FILED _____

STREET ADD _____

AMT/MTG _____

COMMENTS _____

_____

REQUEST FOR INVOICE

If this cancels an original invoice attach a copy with this request.
Please briefly discribe work done so it may be included in billing!
If there are special circumstances please indicate on form.

FIRM PHONE # (this is their acct #) —————————————————————————

NAME OF PERSON TO BILL————————————————————————————

FIRM ————————————————————————————————————

ADDRESS ——————————————————————————————————

CITY/STATE/ZIP ————————————————————————————————

PO# OR BILLING INFO ————————————————————————————

CASE # ————————————————————————————————————

SUBJECT ——————————————————————————————————

WORK DONE ————————————————————————————————

FLATRATE INVESTIGATION CHARGE (type) _____ $ _____

INVESTIGATIVE HOURS ———————— AT $_____ PER HOUR $ _____

MILEAGE: _____ MILES AT $.40 PER MILE $ _____

OFFICIAL RECORDS ——————————————————————————— $ _____

COMPUTER LINE CHARGES ————————————————————————— $ _____

EXPENSES (DETAIL) —————————————————————————————— $ _____

OTHER (EXPLAIN) ———————————————————————————————— $ _____

COMMENTS _____

_____

_____

BRANCH OR DIVISION TO CREDIT:

_____

_____

_____

09\27\ft.INVREQ

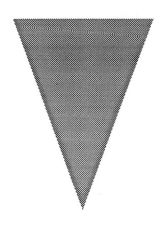

Bibliography

Anderson, Kingdon P. *Undercover Operations: A Manual for the Private Investigator*. Boulder, CO: Paladin Press, 1988.

Blye-Irwin. *Secrets of a Private Eye: Or How to Be Your Own Private Investigator*. New York: H. Holt & Co., 1987.

Bruno, Bob. *Serious Surveillance for the Private Investigator*. Boulder, CO: Paladin Press, 1992.

Fallis, Greg and Ruth Greenberg. *Be Your Own Detective*. New York: M. Evans and Company, 1989.

Faron, Fay. *Take the Money and Strut*. San Francisco: Creighton-Morgan Publishing Group, 1988.

Glossbrenner, Alfred. *How to Look It Up Online*. New York: St. Martin's Press, 1987.

Hoyer, Frederick C,. Jr. *Find Them Fast, Find Them Now: Private Investigators Share Their Secrets for Finding Missing Persons*. Carol Publishing Group, 1988.

Internal Revenue Service. *IRS Manual* (special agent handbook). Washington: U.S. Government Printing Office.

Investigative Reporters and Editors, Inc. *The Reporter's Handbook: An Investigator's Guide to Documents and Techniques*. New York: St. Martin's Press, 1983.

Kizorek, Bill. *Disability of Deception.* Naperville, IL: PSI Publications.

_____ . *Psychological Claims Investigation.* Naperville, IL: PSI Publications.

Lesko, Matthew. *Information USA.* New York: Viking-Penguin, 1986.

Parkhurst, William. *True Detectives: The Real World of Today's Private Investigator.* 1992.

Patterson, William. *Detective's Private Investigation Manual.* Boulder, CO: Paladin Press, 1979.

Pileggi, Nicholas. *Blye, Private Eye.* New York: Pocket Books, 1987.

Royal, Robert, and Steven Schutt. *The Gentle Art of Interviewing and Interrogation.* Englewood Cliffs, NJ: Prentice-Hall, 1976.

Rush, D.A. *Fundamentals of Civil & Private Investigations.* C.C. Thomas, 1984.

Slade, E. Roy. *Sweet Talking: The Pretext Book.* Austin, TX: Thomas Publications, 1986.

Smith, Edward R. *Practical Guide for Private Investigators.* Boulder, CO: Paladin Press, 1982.

Thomas, Ralph. *The Practice of Private Investigation.* Austin, TX: Thomas Publications, Inc.

U.S. Department of the Treasury. *Federal Law Enforcement Training Center, Criminal Investigator Training Division: Sources of Information.* Washington: Government Printing Office, 1990.

Williams, David C. *Investigator's Guide to Sources of Information.* Washington: U.S. Government Printing Office, 1988.

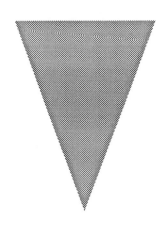

About the Author

Edmund J. Pankau is the founder and president of Intertect, Inc., a Houston-based national private investigation agency. He has more than 20 years of investigative experience, both as a special agent in the U.S. Treasury Intelligence Division and as a private investigator specializing in corporate, legal, and financial investigations.

An accomplished speaker, Pankau conducts seminars throughout the United States on fraud examination, hidden asset location, and the new technology of the private investigator. He has authored numerous articles and has been featured in such publications as the *Wall Street Journal, USA Today, New York Times, Time, Playboy*, and *Entrepreneur*. Some of his most famous cases have been featured on "20/20," CNN's "Moneyline," "America's Most Wanted," "Inside Edition," "Donahue," "Geraldo," "Larry King Live!," and "Joan Rivers."

He is the first investigator in America to hold all three professional certifications in his industry: Certified Legal Investigator (CLI),

Certified Fraud Examiner (CFE), and Certified Protection Professional (CPP). He has also served on the advisory board of the Investigators Online Network, is a member of the American Society for Industrial Security insurance fraud committee, and serves on the board of regents of the National Association of Certified Fraud Examiners.

As a nationally recognized authority of investigator standards and technology, Pankau frequently consults as an expert in the field of financial fraud investigation and investigator industry standards.